I once explained that the reason I don't print my lyrics
in my album booklets was because I felt that song
lyrics are best discovered slowly from the singing voice
rather than the written page. I haven't changed my mind
on this matter. This book is more than my collected
lyrics; it is the story of my life written in song.

BELL PRODUCTIONS
110 LIOSMORE, BARNA, GALWAY, IRELAND
+ 353 (0)91 592531
belljohnny@eircom.net
www.johnnyduhan.com

Corsar Books
ISBN 978-0-9555106-1-8
Printed by Alma Pluss

To the Light
Johnny Duhan
Unsung

For Maur & Crew

Special thanks

Paddy Houlahan, John MacKenna, Francis Kennedy, Des Kenny, Liam Thompson, Kevin McNicholas, Ken Bruen, Kevin Byrne, Johan Hoffteenge, Siobhan Hutson, Jessie Lendennie, Elane Conneely, Eoin Devereux, Alexey Kozemjakov, Bruno Staehelin John Ryan, Max & Leo and Tommy Carter. Not forgetting the many singers and bands who have recorded songs from this collection over the years & the musicians who have played on my albums, plus the radio presenters and music critics who have put focus on my work.

Prologue

In a recurring dream I'm on the stage of a large theatre (much larger that the art centres and folk clubs I'm accustomed to performing in), about to start singing to a capacity crowd who have just greeted me with the most enthusiastic round of applause of my career when a fire breaks out at the back of the hall that sends the audience scurrying for the exit doors, leaving me alone and bewildered in a pall of smoke on the stage.

This dream illustrates my deepest fears regarding the performance side of my career. Despite that, I decided to present this book of my collected lyrics in the form of four separate stage performances, mainly because the stories that bind the collections together came to me on stage and seem the most natural way of introducing a reading audience to my work, but also to display my entire life's work in the prism of just four sequential chapters.

The title **To The Light** seemed appropriate on a number of levels, mainly because there is a celebration of light running through my work, starting with my boyhood love of sunlight in **Just Another Town**; my hankering for limelight in **To The Light**; a yearning for the family hearth-glow in **The Voyage**, and finally, my quest for spiritual light in **Flame**.

These four chapters of my unsung story offer a clear picture of the scope of the lyrical side of my design, but another aim in producing this book was to try and awaken interest in my musical albums, for it is the melodies charging my words that transform lyrics into song.

Introduction to Chapter One

Just Another Town is a portrait of the city I grew up in. It sings of the people and location that formed me. Its melody and poetry come from the homes, bars, dancehalls, chapels, gardens, prisons, factories, and the very streets of the town it celebrates.

It is not a nostalgic look back in blinkered pleasure. The landscape is urban, gritty and hard, and the characters are flawed and damaged.

DH Lawrence once described towns as "scabs" on the face of the earth before he attempted to flee back to some primitive idyll. Modern cities are indeed scabs on the face of the world, but the way I see it, scabs are healing skin formations in the process of transforming damaged tissue back into healthy flesh. One of the greatest achievements of mankind, I believe, is that we have learned to live in relative harmonious community in vast cities all over the world in a relatively short space of time.

A spiritual dimension lies behind the ordering process that has brought about this transformation. **Just Another Town** attempts to illustrate some of the elements and forces that bound together the fragile community I grew up with. It also shows how youthful innocence can act as a compass to guide us in doubting times.

Chapter One

Just Another Town

While climbing a timberstack in Limerick's
dockyard as a boy, a splinter pierced my hand.
As well as the throb of pain I also recall a clear blue
sky mirrored in the Shannon and the sweet smell
of woodbeams stacked along the wharf where my
father's freighter was moored with raised flag,
ready to sail.

Just Another Town opens with the sound of a horn heralding Another Morning. Living as our family did close to Limerick's army barracks, the horn is significant as I recall being woken on many occasions in my youth by the echo of the dawn reveille coming down Barrack-hill. The room into which the sound and sunlight seeped was a tiny bedroom that I shared with three brothers, all crammed into a set of two-tiered bunks; Michael and Barry at either end on the bottom and Eric on top. Being the eldest boy (I was twelve or thirteen at the time recalled in the song) I had the privilege of a single bed all to myself.

The first thing that faced me each morning when I woke was a framed print of Our Lady of Fatima, to whom my mother was devoted. The walls were also decorated with a variety of oil and watercolour paintings by my brother Eric, and the ceiling was outlined with the contours of Michelangelo's *Creation of Adam* Sistine mural etched in charcoal by my brother Michael, who was devoted to the great Florentine master and happy to share part of his name.

Though surrounded by my brothers' first artistic endeavours, my opening song doesn't focus on them. The light gleaming through the narrow framed window and the sights, sounds and smells coming in from the awakening town outside, these are the remembered elements that fired my blood with the lust to be up and out in the thick of it, where bells were ringing, neighbours were chatting and humming, and where, most important of all, young girls would soon be out and about in their bright school uniforms.

I had all the worries of adolescence, but on
such mornings as this – and I remember lots
of them – the sheer brilliance of the summer
sun melted all care away.

Another Morning

Outside the sun has announced another morning,
It's red and warming, I feel it in my bed.
Down in the street I can hear people walking,
I hear them talking; they mumble in my head.

The sun is shining down on the city,
The sky is clear and blue.
Girls going to school will look pretty,
It's time I was up too.

I can smell someone's breakfast frying
While I'm lying, looking at the sky;
And I can see a plane flying, its trail dying
While I watch it fly.

The sun is shining down on the city,
The sky is clear and blue.
Girls going to school will look pretty,
It's time I was up too.

I can hear a church bell ringing
And someone singing somewhere in the street;
Outside the sun has announced another morning,
It's red and warming, I can feel the heat.

The chorus-call to life of Another Morning draws the boy out-doors to confront the harsher aspects of city living set out in Always Remember, but with the memory of his initial optimism buoying him up for the ordeal.

Town planning has always fascinated me. While I was attending the Christian Brothers National School on Sexton Street, just up the road from the Pig Factory, I noticed from one of the top story windows of the main grey building that the school was in close proximity to some of the grimmest structures in the city - Limerick Jail, St. Joseph's Mental Hospital and Mount St Lawrence's Cemetery, all juxtaposed one after the other on Mulgrave Street. Think about it! The planners who arranged the town in this order lived no doubt out in the leafy Ennis Road and sent their kids to the Crescent College on pristine O'Connell Avenue for a Jesuit education. Going on the assumption that the Cemetery was the first of these landmarks to be allocated its place out in hidden valley, we can only surmise that when the time arrived to build the city's mental asylum the planners put on their thinking caps in an effort to locate the most tranquil site for housing disturbed mental patients and - wait for it - fixed on the plot beside the graveyard. The same rationale probably applied to the placement of the city jail. Imagine the city councillors and planners scratching their heads over the location for this towering, barbed wired edifice.

"Where should we put it?" asks Councillor John, to which alderman Mike replies: "What about that grand site beside the mental hospital just down the road from the graveyard. When the prisoners gaze through the iron bars of their cells they'll have a grand view of the mental patients louring at the headstones, and that'll give the blackguards something to think about!" Finally, when the Christian Brothers arrived with their scheme for helping the town's poorer classes get an education, the town planners facilitated them in their usual altruistic way by handing over the prime site close to the Pig Factory, the jail, the mental hospital and the graveyard.

Always Remember

Surrounded by factories and prisons,
Surrounded by drunken barrooms;
By homes full of divisions
And graveyards full of tombs.

But somewhere between the anguish and pain
We learned to find our fun;
Somewhere between the clouds and the rain
We always remembered the sun.

Surrounded by barracks and schools,
Surrounded by slums of the poor;
By the courthouse applying the rules
And hospitals searching for cures.

But somewhere between the anguish and pain
We learned to find our fun;
Somewhere between the clouds and the rain
We always remembered the sun.

Surrounded by homes for the crippled,
Surrounded by homes for the blind,
By homes for the deaf and dumb people
And people going out of their minds.

But somewhere between all the anguish and pain
We learned to find our fun,
Somewhere between the clouds and rain
We always remembered the sun.
O always remember the sun.

Despite the bleak realities of city life, kids have a way of making the most of things. I guess that's why Christ set them up as role models. But the fun they manage to squeeze out of the mundane isn't always that innocent.

Recently, I was sitting in our living-room running over a new song when I glanced through the front window and noticed our twelve year old daughter Ailbhe with her friend Sara-Kate in a nearby playground. A few minutes later I looked out again and five other kids from a neighbouring estate had joined them, three of whom I noted were boys, one at least fifteen. The fifteen year old - a good-looking kid sporting a bleached semi-Mohican hairstyle - gave me a moment's pause as I realised I had seen him in Barna Woods a week or so before, lying in a bed of leaves with a young girl, ghetto blaster pumping rap behind their heaving bodies.

After bringing this to mind, I peered through the window again and noticed that the playground was empty. I rushed out to investigate.

Following a path that leads to a copse of alders close to where we live, I came to a narrow, down-hill track that meanders through some high grass and dense foliage. Three quarters way down the slope I came upon my ten year old son, Brian, and his Indian friend Rohit crouched behind some tall fronds of bracken, peering towards the trees at the bottom of the hill. Noticing me, the boys tried to bolt for it but I caught Brian by the arm and asked him what they were up to. Brian pointed towards a clearing in the woods where the gang were standing with their backs to us. Spotting Ailbhe in the group, I asked Brian what they were up to. Brian hesitated then tittered, "Talking about sex."

Calling Ailbhe's name at the top of my voice, I ordered her straight home. And when we got back to the house I gave her a stern lecture on the dangers of going to isolated places with members of the opposite sex. Half way through my rant she laughed and reminded me of my next song.

In the Garden

In the autumn evenings
We used to creep to our Eden -
An avenue garden - when the moon bloomed.
There was Carol and Annie, and Bobby and Brenny,
And Bobby had many ideas on how to please;
He would tease the girls when they'd freeze
And put them at ease.

We'd hug them and rub them,
Even though we didn't love them;
We were young then, so young then,
We weren't sure what we were doing in the garden.

In the grass we'd be sitting,
Sitting and kissing,
Bobby and Annie; Carol, Brenny and me.
And we'd be swapping as night would be dropping;
Bobby'd take Carol while Brenny and me
Quite innocently would share Annie.

We hugged them and rubbed them
Even though we didn't love them.
We were young then, so young then,
We weren't sure then what we were doing
In the Garden.

I had a falling out with the record company who put up the initial finance to produce the first edition of **Just Another Town** because they tried to dictate that the collection should start with the title track, to maximise its airplay potential. I could see their logic but I had a clear concept that the album should open with a song heralding the summer sun coming up and close with a ballad carolling the rising of a winter moon. While the stand-off with the company was going on I had a revealing dream in which I was standing in a field of golden corn (my song harvest) when the faint sound of a gun blast (my record company's ultimatum) startled thousands of birds into sudden flight, filling the sky with a mass of flapping wings. As I awoke I drew a sigh of relief knowing that the gun-shot had been too far off to inflict mortal damage.

The record company dropped me but, soon after, I had another dream in which I was half way across a flimsy narrow bridge - petrified that I might slip in and drown - when I lost my footing and fell into two feet of shallow water. After this awakening I invested my own finance in completing **Just Another Town** in my own fashion, and I went on from there to produce all my other work in the same independent way. Compromise in everything except art.

The opening line of the title song, Just Another Town, features a disturbed spinster who lived up the street from us on Wolfe Tone Street, across from where the old synagogue used to be. This unfortunate woman suffered from manic depression from her late teens after her widowed father (it was said) prevented her from marrying a common sailor on the grounds that he was socially beneath her. The old man – a grumpy octogenarian who always seemed to have food stains on his shirt-fronts – sold apples to the neighbourhood kids from a small orchard at the back of their house. When we called with our pennies he would take us into the back garden and allow us to point out the fruit of our choice and then knock it from the trees with a long wooden pole. His daughter rarely appeared and, whenever she did, she stayed silently in the shadowy background (the house and garden teemed with shadows), dressed in dark tones. One evening, however, when I called alone with a single copper coin in my palm she answered the front door and stepped into the twilight with a livid expression on her pinched face and started ranting and raving about how she had seen my sister Joan showing her knickers to some boys on a piece of waste ground called Gabbit's Field the evening before. Though I couldn't make head nor tail of the sexual innuendo in her charge, I knew by the molten look in her eyes that something serious was amiss. Luckily her father heard the commotion and came to the door twisting his hands (a bright yellow egg stain on his tie always comes back with the memory). After ushering her into a dark room off the hallway he hurriedly conducted me into the back garden and let me pick two apples for my penny instead of the usual one.

There was always something going on in the street.
Young kids playing hopscotch, older kids playing poker;
drunks staggering from the pubs, cripples hobbling on
crutches; widows in black going to the chapel, girls in
bright dresses going to the dance. There was a lot there
to be disturbed about, but on certain summer evenings
when the sun was going down and the brass band was
practising up the hill, I wouldn't have wanted to be
anywhere else

Just Another Town

The old spinster is going insane.
Her next door neighbour is in church again.
Two drunks are fighting down in the lane
While little children are playing a game.

Dogs are barking, little girls sing,
And the chapel bell begins to ring.
Someone deals Bobby a King;
On the pavement money starts to ring.

And the street is drifting into evening
While the sun is going down.
I'm just back there capturing the feeling
Though it's just another town,
Just another town.

The cripple crawls up the avenue.
Someone else says, "How do you do?"
Someone kicks a ball over to you
While the sky begins to lose its hue.

A group of old stevedores from the ships
Come up the street bent from the hips;
One takes a cigarette from his lips.
Someone else drops the coin he flips.

And the street is drifting into evening
While the sun is going down.
I'm just back there capturing the feeling
Though it's just another town,
Just another town.

And in the band-room up on the hill
A brass band's playing, I can hear it still –
The slide trombone is softly blown.

The old nurse is on her way to the shops.
The epileptic suddenly drops.
Down the hill my father's in the docks.
In the bar the drinking never stops.

Bobby throws down a pair of queens.
The church bell interrupts someone's dreams.
Someone's talking of football teams.
Some girl is straightening her nylon seams.

And the street is drifting into evening
While the sun is going down.
I'm just back there capturing the feeling
Though it's just another town,
Just another town.

There were three pubs on our street, and all three did thriving business. One was owned by a friend of my mother's - Mrs R - who gave me a Sunday morning job when I was thirteen, cleaning glasses and sweeping the floor after the busiest night of the week. Mrs R – a stout woman with a sweet tooth and a sweet smile - paid me generously and let me keep any small change I found on the floor.

During my second morning on the job, I stole ten Gold Flake cigarettes from a shelf behind the counter (I'd just started smoking and the temptation was too much for me). Though my conscience came at me when the fags ran out, I repeated the theft the following Sunday and I also stole two copper coins from the till while I was at it. Though my conscience pricked me harder than ever all that week, I attempted an even bigger heist the following Sunday.

While I was rummaging for a silver sixpence among the pennies Mrs R came into the bar unexpectedly and caught me with my hand in the till. Her smile dissolved instantly and was replaced by a look of grave disappointment. She didn't say anything, just looked deep into my eyes and then turned on her heels and let me get on with my act of treachery.

During the following agonising days I waited for her to inform my mother, but she didn't tell her. I never went back to the bar, but a couple of months later I overheard my mother telling my father that Mrs R had been diagnosed with chronic diabetes by her GP.

Confession (After Villon)

When Mrs R caught me
With my fingers in her till
Her eyes lost all their sweet lustre.
She was diagnosed diabetic soon after
And her sweet tooth
Was deprived of all sugar.
She died a year later.
But that was forty years ago,
So why this cogitation? –
I was just a petty thief
Not a murderer.

When I was nine or ten, my uncle Jim (one of Mrs R's best customers) took me to a carnival on a piece of waste ground on O'Connell Avenue to see a daredevil diving from what seemed a colossal height into a blazing tank of oily water. More than Bill Haley, Del Shannon or Buddy Holly (early idols), it was this daredevil who first put the notion of a career in show-business in my head. I was so impressed by his performance I attended every one of his nightly shows and even went along to a matinee he gave on the Sunday before the carnival departed town. In the full light of day without a starry backdrop, the illusion of his death-defying act wasn't quite as impressive. As he climbed the narrow ladder up into the blue dome of day a number of gaping holes could be detected in his black leotards around the crotch area, and the steps he ascended to a fanfare of rattling snare drums didn't appear to stretch quite as high into the afternoon heavens as they did at night. Still, when he set himself alight at the top of the ladder and plunged meteor-like into the flaming pool, the roar of the crowd went up just as loud as ever.

Daredevil

I'm up here where the night is star-freckled;
The moon on my head is a lily petal;
And a thousand eyes are looking up at me;
Will I stay alive, that's what they're waiting to see.

I'm employed in a carnival;
I climb high to dare the devil;
Aflame in the sky, like a bird I fly,
And when I dive they sigh, "Will he die?"

I'm up higher than the cross on the steeple;
The moon is my halo; I'm like Jesus to these people.
But now I understand why the devil couldn't tempt him;
I'm up here just to suit a devilish whim.

I'm employed in a carnival,
I climb high to dare the devil;
Aflame in the sky, like a bird I fly,
And when I dive they sigh, "Will he die?"

And so I keep going higher and higher
While the devil stays below in the pool of fire,
And the tongues of flame are laughing up at me -
"You're going to miss the pool," that's what they're saying
to me.

If that Daredevil turned my life upsidedown, Uncle Jim's life was already topsy-turvy from the drink by this stage. Neglecting his family, he went on a permanent binge, staggering from pub to pub and getting into all sorts of trouble in the process. On one occasion he was picked up in his underwear on the main street, waving a stolen brolly at the shocked community. My father spent years bailing him out of fix after fix and finding him jobs he never held down for longer than a day, till eventually he gave up on him. One of the saddest days in my youth was watching my father turning his own drunken brother away from our house and warning him never to darken our door again.

I loved this man, an ex sailor. He was like a fish out of water in this world. He once walked O'Connell Street in his shorts for a wager, but on another occasion I saw the more desperate side of his nature when I visited him in a cell.

Let's Just Have Another Drink

Let's just have another drink, we'll talk about the past.
Let's just have another round, we'll make this one our last.
My wife will be annoyed with me when I arrive home drunk,
But my spirit feels so sunk.

I used to be a sailor, sailed on many ships;
I travelled all around the world, used to love those trips.
But I disobeyed many orders while I was at sea;
The captain sacked me.

I came home and got a job here in the town.
The work wasn't heavy but the routine weighed me down;
Each day seemed so endless, it drove me round the bend;
I left there in the end.

Then things went from bad to worse, couldn't find
                                another job,
At least one I could hold on to, I started to rob.
This landed me in jail, they put me in a cell
Where the loneliness was hell.

I've always had a restless soul, nothing seems to suit me;
Out of tune with the world and full of self-pity.
Soon I'm going to make a change, just you wait and see,
But now have this drink with me.

O let's just have another drink, one more for the road.
Just one more for the road.

Down the road from the bar where Jim did most of his drinking, I was playing handball with Bobby O'Connor against Beegan's gable one evening when bells started ringing for Benediction. My mother called me from our terraced house up the street and asked me to attend the service for "a special intention". Being three score ahead in the game, I did everything in my power to get out of the obligation but my mother's appealing eyes got the better of me. After some huffing and puffing, I stuffed the ball in my pocket and went along to the chapel, dragging Bobby with me.

The choir was in full flight when we arrived at St Joseph's, singing a favourite hymn of mine, Hail Queen of Heaven, which I associated with my father away at sea.

As we took a pew near the back of the church Bobby observed that we were the youngest people in the chapel. All around us elderly men and women, bent over beads and missals, were mumbling prayers and coughing and sniffling. Soon after the priest started the exotic service, Bobby asked me in a whisper what the "sun-like thing" between the candles was for, and while I was explaining the function of the monstrance, an old man with a bulbous purple nose sitting in front of us turned and silenced me with a sibilant spray of sour spittle: "Shhhhhh!"

Later in the service, while the priest was swinging the thurible in front of the altar, spreading incense in preparation for the adoration, Bobby nudged me again, asking me what was going on, but I ignored him this time and lowered my head for the raising of the encased host. As the sweet smell of incense reached our nostrils, the choir above our heads broke into a soaring hymn that I hadn't heard before. The melody was so pure and intense it sent shivers down my spine. I looked around the chapel at all the bent withered old people singing along with cracked voices and tears began welling up in my eyes. I can't recall the name of the hymn but I tried to recapture some of its essence in my next song.

Benediction

Bells were ringing, ringing out in the town,
In the evening when the light died down;
And I remember people going along -
When the congregation was strong - for benediction,
The rising of the Son – benediction -
The rising of the Son, in benediction.

A choir was singing, singing clear and soft,
Voices weaving hymns in the organ loft,
And I remember people kneeling down,
Humble people of the town – for benediction –

The rising of the Son – benediction –
The rising of the Son, in benediction.

Through clouds of incense
The golden monstrance
Shining so bright in candlelight,
Showing God's might in benediction.

Many of my earliest memories are full of aspects of the sacred, though a few of theses are tinged with elements of the romantic as well. For instance, I was a daily mass goer during Lent but spent as much time eyeing Ann Flanagan in her maroon Laurel Hill school uniform as I did praying.

Another girl I fell for in a big way at this time was Patsy H. Patsy was a stunning blond with a long swinging pony-tail, but she was off limits to me on a number of counts; she lived *up* the hill in a much larger house than ours; she was Protestant and mixed in different circles; and she seemed much taller than I was from a distance. Despite these seemingly insurmountable obstacles, I did manage to have one dramatic dalliance with Patsy in adolescence.

It was on the afternoon of an Air Display that was due to take place in the skies above the army barracks. On the day in question – a hot sunny Sunday - Jimmy Hanley invited a gang of us to play Spin the Bottle in his house, while his widowed father was out of town. When we arrived for the session I was over the moon to find that Jimmy had also invited Patsy (his next door neighbour).

On the fifth or sixth bottle-spin, Patsy and I were aligned for a kiss, so we went to the smooching room next door. It was only then that I discovered that the discrepancy in our heights was even greater than I had imagined. While I was awkwardly leaning up to reach her mouth and she was obligingly bending down to make lip contact, our teeth collided, causing us both pain and shame. Luckily when we returned to the kitchen, no one noticed our embarrassment as it was nearing the time when the air display was due to begin.

Putting the milk bottle aside, Jimmy ushered us upstairs to his father's bedroom, which overlooked the barrack grounds. After ten or fifteen minutes of waiting for the gliders to be towed in by engine-driven aircraft from Rineanna Airfield, most of the gang got fed up with mooning around the hot musty bedroom and went off to the shops for ice-pops, leaving Jimmy, Patsy and myself alone in the bedroom.

Sitting on the edge of Jimmy's father's bed, Patsy fanned her face with her hand while Jimmy and I stood by the window scrutinising the empty sky. Glancing back at Patsy's tanned legs, Jimmy gave me a nudge and a wink and openly suggested that I go over and take up where I'd left off downstairs. Patsy didn't object so I made my way over to the bed and stood beside her. She put out her hands and, without fully realising what I was doing, I sat on her lap and put my arms around her. She giggled and offered me her lips, but just as we were about to kiss, Jimmy called out, "Hey, here they come, the gliders!" Patsy pushed me aside and rushed to the window. I followed more limply and looked out at the blue sky.

Four or five small planes were floating around in the heavens like seagulls. Jimmy informed us that the aircraft had no engines and were kept airborne only by the power of the wind. Patsy gasped and pointed to two planes that seemed to be heading straight for a collision. Jimmy said that this was just a manoeuvre, but as the planes passed one another their wings clipped and one of the aircraft started making a rapid descent. Though it happened in an instant, time seemed to freeze. Patsy grabbed my arm and started shaking. I stood on my toes but couldn't see beyond a row of galvanised roofs inside the barrack grounds. Jimmy lost his colour and exclaimed, "It must have crash-landed."

We ran downstairs and out into the street where a number of people were standing with shocked faces pointing towards Edward Street.

Leaving Patsy with her mouth agape, Jimmy and I ran as fast as we could up Calooney Street and around the corner. A minute or so later we came upon the wreckage, a pile of debris scattered like matchwood by the gable of a house facing a parcel of land containing a grotto to Our Lady.

Because a large group was standing around the scene of

the accident it was impossible to see what condition the pilot was in but an old lady standing nearby kept muttering in a tearful voice, "He's dead, God love him; he's dead." A man with a white face shuffled back from the crowd and confirmed that the pilot was indeed dead, asking for someone to phone for an ambulance. But an ambulance was already on its way; its high pitched siren drawing nearer and nearer, intensifying the sense of tragedy in the air.

An old man pointed his walking stick towards the grotto and cleared his throat. "If he'd crashed there he might have had a chance but there was a group of children playing near the statue so he steered towards the gable instead. A brave man!"

An old woman in a black shawl took a pair of rosary-beads from the pocket of her navy apron and started saying a Hail Mary. We all joined in.

Mary

O Mary, it's true I loved you
But it's been so long I'd forgotten you.
You dressed in blue and white too
And my memory picks daffodils for you;
In a park in the city I stole them for you,
Now those flowers remind me of you;
When I went to a park when the spring was new
A bunch of those memories grew, that's true,
So I picked a bunch and thought of you.

O Mary, it's true I left you
For someone I thought more real than you.
Yeah Mary, I grew and I threw
Away all those memories of you,
Till I went to a park when the spring was new
Then a bunch of those memories grew;
In a park in the city I stole them for you,
Now those flowers remind me of you, it's true,
So I picked a bunch and thought of you.

From an early age we were encouraged by our religious teachers – first the nuns on Henry Street and later the Brothers on Sexton Street - to bring flowers for the Marian shrines that were decked out in our class-rooms. The shrines usually consisted of no more than a medium sized blue and white statue of Our Lady mounted on a box covered with coloured paper or tinfoil and surrounded by a few nightlight candles and a selection of jam-jars for flowers.

The most impressive of these altars that I remember was one that Brother Dom assembled while I was in sixth class. Brother Dom, one of the cruellest men I have met in my life, must have had great devotion to our Lady for he was continually coaxing us to bring fresh flowers so as not to sully the Virgin with wilted and withered petals. Between humiliating us with cruel insults about our low intelligence and flogging us to within an inch of our lives for minor offences, Brother Dom always softened for the Angelus at midday, after which he would make his gentle appeal for late daffodils, fresh bluebells and early roses. After he gave me a particularly bad beating one day for not putting a penny in the Black Baby box (I had one in my pocket but refused to give it under duress) I showed my parents the weals left on my arms and legs. My father accompanied me to school the next day and confronted the principal, Brother Biggs, with me by his side. Brother Biggs glanced at the red marks still visible on my limbs but refused to take any action against Brother Dom. Dismissing my father with a wave of the hand he tried to turn his back on us but my father caught him by the shoulder and asked him to take off his collar and come outside. Biggs didn't take up the challenge. He stammered and stuttered and then slinked away with his tail between his legs.

Though my father attended mass with the family each Sunday, he didn't believe in the Virgin birth or in life after death (two of the most fundamental tenets of the Catholic faith). "When I die," he used to quip after he'd had a few, "don't waste money on a funeral; just dump me in a dustbin and chuck me in the Shannon." By the time I reached adolescence I had heard this mantra so often I began to have religious doubts myself.

Coupled with the scepticism inherited from my father, I was also drawn away from the restrictions of the faith by the common hormonal urge of adolescence. Living as we did near Limerick's Red Light District (three pubs on the Dock Road), I learned early about the dark wiles of sex. While the congregation of devout elders would be limping to evening Benediction, they would often rub shoulders with – and look down their noses at - prostitutes from a near-by council estate who had to pass through our street to get to their workplace in the docks. From the pavement by Beegan's gable, Bobby, Brenny and I would ogle their waggling behinds and speculate on what they got up to with their sailor customers in the dockland bars. A constant daydream of mine at this time was to live in a world free of the law of chastity. But I wasn't alone in feeling this. This was the early '60s when the collective subconscious was gearing up for the sexual revolution that would eventually lead us all to the nirvana we're surviving today.

Two Minds

I can hear sirens down in the harbour;
I can hear chapel bells ringing louder;
I'm back many years ago on a street I know
By a corner, my thoughts in disorder.

I can see the chapel's tall steeple
On the hill as a holy symbol,
Like a rocket to be launched to heaven
If I step aboard at seven
With the people heading for the steeple.

And the congregation going up the hill
Are all dressed up for the invisible saviour.
The countdown is ringing in my ear;
A choir is waiting to sing there for the saviour,
And I'm in two minds about where to go –
The church on the hill or the harbour below.

I can see a ship coming up the river
With a halo of gulls squealing overhead her;
It's just back from some paradise,
All the sailors will be singing tonight in the harbour
And I'm in a fever

'Cause there's prostitutes coming down the street
All dressed up for sailors they'll meet in the harbour.
Sirens are ringing in my ear;
Soon the sailors will be drinking beer in the harbour.
And I'm in two minds about where to go -
The church on the hill or the harbour below.

I can hear sirens down in the harbour.
I can hear the chapel bells ringing louder;
I'm back many years ago on a street I know
By a corner, my thoughts in disorder.

And the congregation, still going up the hill,
Are all dressed up for the invisible saviour.
And prostitutes coming down the street
Are all dressed up for sailors they'll meet
                              in the harbour.
And I'm in two minds about where to go -
The church on the hill or the harbour below.

After seeing the film version of Robert Louis Stevenson's *Treasure Island* when I was nine or ten, a friend and I tried to stowaway on a Norwegian freighter but we were caught in the hold by one of the crew and marched before a stern-faced skipper who demanded an explanation in broken English for what we were doing on in his ship. Without blinking an eye – I was always good at coming up with lies in tricky situations - I told the irate captain that we were looking for my father, which wasn't such a lie after all.

Stowaway

I used to go to the dockyard
To watch the big ships coming in;
I'd mingle with sailors,
Some my own kin,
And dream of being a stowaway,
Dream of going far away
Down the river, all the way,
And out into the Ocean.

I'd climb a stack of timber
That the ships had brought in;
I'd sit and smell the fresh wood,
Listening to the dock din,
And dream of being a stowaway;
Dream of going far away
Down the river, all the way,
Out into the ocean.

The whole world out there turning
Had me dizzy as a boy;
My heart was burning for joy.

I used to walk down the dockyard
To see the big ships going out;
I'd watch them growing smaller
With an open mouth,
And dream of being a stowaway,
Dream of going far away,
Down the river, all the way
And out into the ocean.

I haunted the docks as a kid, waiting for my father's
ship to come in. I had romantic notions of his life on
the open sea, fed by tall tales that he himself spun to my
brothers and me on cold winter nights in front of the fire
when he was home on leave.

Telemacus (son of Ulysses)

At sea again or docked in some port town,
On leave, maybe dancing to a calypso in some girl's arms,
My mother said he was quite a dancer then.

When she took me shopping
I often wondered why she smiled
When young men whistled as we passed.

At night she knit ganseys by the fireside
Where ornaments from China gleamed,
Brass dragons on the mantelpiece.

Her needles clicked like chopsticks
Picking up wool noodle; she fed her dreams
On reams and reams of plain and purl.

Scarves and mittens too digested a little of her sorrow
And kept her hoping that my father's ship
Might be hooked at the end of her line of wool.

After school I went to the docks,
Mingled with sailors, sat on timber stacks
And dreamed of being a stowaway.

I thought of my father then as a conquistador,
But he was just a slack-black stoker
Melting for furnace flames, for steam - the blood of his ship.

I didn't fully realise the implications
Of a world made round,
Of the raised flag at the tip of the icy pole.

In undiscovered lands my imagined banners flew
In the kitchen where my mother's knitting
Like a shroud of sorrow grew,

While out at sea my father hoisted
On his strained shovel
The death-flag of my youngest dreams.

Due to family commitments (all eight of us – four girls and four boys), my father gave up going to sea when I was ten or eleven and took a job as a maintenance engineer in a clothing factory, but he still went to Joe's Bar on Henry Street where the old sea-dog fraternity did their drinking. Often on autumn and winter evenings he would take me along with him when he went for his customary couple of pints after work, and most nights he would be called on for a song. He always obliged. Ramona was a favourite but he also had a number of songs like Keep Right On Till the End of The Road that dealt with holding up the spirits in tough times. With lyrics like this in mind, I wrote the following ballad, a song for Everyman that I'm sure my father would have made a great fist of singing.

This Time

This time he feels he'll have success,
He feels it in his bones,
Even though his life's a mess
And hope is all he owns;
He keeps on going, carries on,
And tries to find a way;
Keeps alive a light that shone
On him in better days.

The light is dim but it will shine again,
Hope will make it shine deep in him.
The light is dim but it will shine again,
It will shine again on him.

This time he feels confident
That he won't go astray,
Almost feels it provident
That things will be okay;
His faith is strong, his doubt is gone;
His spirit's in command.
Though it's still night he looks upon,
He feels the dawn at hand.

The light is dim but it will shine again,
Hope will make it shine deep in him.
The light is dim but it will shine again,
It will shine again on him.

Up until my teens, my big dream in life was to become a sailor like my father. Then I discovered rhythm and blues and the dream changed overnight.

When I was fifteen I went to Dublin with a few friends to attend a Rolling Stones' concert. Along with our pre-booked concert tickets we each had just enough money, wrangled from our parents, for food and a B&B for the overnight stay.

Before searching for accommodation, we went window-shopping for "mod gear" and I spotted a green and red pair of plaid hipsters that I had to try on. Once I got them on I didn't want to take them off, so I decided to fork out my B&B money and rough it for the night. Luckily, one of the others who had taken a shine to a purple shirt with elephant collars followed my example, so I had a partner in my foolishness. The others told us that we were mad to do this but we ignored them.

After the concert my accomplice and I tried to sneak into the other boys' B&B on the Quays but the landlady's eagle-eyes made it impossible. After an hour or more of trudging around the vicinity of Christchurch we flopped down on the pavement of a side street and tried unsuccessfully to go to sleep huddled together on the cold concrete. An elderly passer-by took pity on us and advised us to go to St Vincent de Paul's Night Shelter for the homeless, giving us directions on how to get there. Twenty minutes later we arrived at the building and the custodians reluctantly took us in. We were given separate cubicles in a large dormitory full of sniffling and coughing men, but we were grateful to be in off the streets.

The following morning - after a few fitful hours of sleep - we attended mass and breakfasted with a ragged congregation of tramps and down-and-outs. Some of them were very disturbed and sad looking characters but others seemed just normal men down on their luck.

Though I remember little of the Rolling Stones' concert, the experience of rubbing shoulders with real rolling stones haunted me for years.

One Hundred Miles

One hundred miles from his home
Through a lonely city he roams
Till he finds a bed he doesn't own
In a house for rolling stones.

There he can lay his head down;
There he can relax his frown.
There he can dream of his hometown,
In his sleep his troubles drown.

But when he wakes up and takes his first look
At his tattered surroundings;
When he awakes, when his dream breaks
He asks himself, "How can I survive
Another day of being alive
Till evening comes?"

One hundred miles from his home,
He has nothing left to call his own,
Just the rags for his bones
And the memory of his home.

As he gets out of the bed
Sadness starts to cloud his head;
His heart fills with dread,
He almost wishes he were dead.

For when he wakes up and takes his first look
At his tattered surroundings,
When he awakes, when his dream breaks
He asks himself, "How can I survive
Another day of being alive
Till the evening comes?"

35

Just before I released the first edition of **Just Another Town**, I began to have reservations about some of the songs on the album, fearing that the subject matter of three of the lyrics in particular – mental illness (Everything Will Be Alright), alcoholism (Let's Just Have Another Drink) and homelessness (One Hundred Miles) – might lessen the album's commercial appeal. After agonising on the matter of whether I should drop one or more of these songs from the collection, I made up a batch of demo copies to send to friends for advice and went off to Galway's town centre to mail them.

On my way to the GPO on Eglinton Street - it was a hot sticky summer's afternoon and the place was teaming with tourists and shoppers - I noticed a man in the middle of the road obstructing traffic and shouting obscenities at passers-by. The man was clearly mentally unbalanced but the passing drivers and pedestrians were so irked by the heat of the day and the traffic congestion, they didn't take this into consideration. Several irate drivers rolled down their windows and cursed the poor devil openly while a bald-headed old timer passing me called the man a "fruitcake".

Preoccupied as I was with my own concerns, I pressed on to the Post Office. After posting my batch of demos I decided to drop into the Franciscan chapel on my way home to say a quick prayer for guidance on the issue of the doubtful songs. As I approached the church I noticed a wino slouched on the steps of the portico with his back against a granite pillar, wine bottle in hand, blabbering to himself. A group of girls in school uniforms from a nearby convent were laughing at him and several church-goers threw disparaging looks his way as they entered the church. Noticing the black pigment of his sunken face, I looked away and went on into the chapel. Leaving the church minutes later I noticed the wino offering his bottle to an incensed old lady who was rebuking him for "defiling the house of God". The old dear glanced at me for support but I hurried past her, eager to get home to start working on a song in progress.

Despite my enthusiasm for work, the new lyric failed to ignite so I knocked off early and went for a walk to the Corrib river. On my way down the Dyke Road I came upon a tramp with a shaggy mongrel standing outside the Simon Shelter for the homeless. As I approached, he asked me if I thought the shelter would object to him taking in his dog for the night. I glanced at the mongrel and suggested that he go in and ask, telling him that the Simon Community were a very sympathetic organisation. He thanked me and I walked on.

A few moments later on the path leading to the river - still thinking about the songs - I found myself muttering a prayer, asking God to send me some kind of guiding spirit to show me what to do. While I was talking to myself, I was interrupted by the sound of a dog barking behind my back. I swung round and found the tramp and his dog standing a few feet away. I laughed to hide my embarrassment. The tramp explained that he was taking his dog for a swim. We walked to the river together and carried on a brief conversation while the dog retrieved a stick from the flow.

Soon after I reached home – while I was back struggling with my new song - it suddenly dawned on me that the three characters I had encountered during the course of day - the mentally ill man, the drunk and the tramp - corresponded exactly with the subjects of the three songs on **Just Another Town** that I was having doubts about. Needless to say, I left all three of the songs on the first edition of the album and added another few dark ones to the second edition, for true measure.

Behind the big house on the site where the old synagogue used to be on Calooney Street (or *Little Jerusalem,* as it was once called) the owner started building a yacht. On spring and summer evenings the sound of his hammer echoing around the neighbourhood brought Noah to mind. Months of drilling and hammering went by and slowly the boat began to take shape. Often when the family were away we would sneak a look at the craft through the iron bars of the gate at the side of the house. As big as the house was, the boat seemed even bigger. When it was completed it looked magnificent – perfectly shaped in narrow beams of honey-coloured wood with gleaming silver fixtures and a snow-white furled sail tied up with leather thongs on the lowered spar above the cabin porthole. A professional boat-builder at the top of his skills wouldn't have made a better job of the vessel. Studying it through the bars, we speculated on how many people the cabin might hold and how high the mast would be when erected.

Eventually, a huge crane arrived in the street and hauled the boat out over the roof of the house and settled it on a jeep-drawn trailer that transported it to a launching ramp on the Shannon. The owner and his family enjoyed many outings on the river. Then one fateful day the owner's son fell overboard in a tragic accident and drowned.

The Shannon took many lives while I was growing up, and not all by accident. A boy older than me who lived up the street from the boat-builder – a lad who couldn't read or write - committed suicide for no apparent reason. Because of the three or four year age difference between us, we weren't close friends but whenever we met we'd nod or smile in passing. Other kids from the neighbourhood who knew of his illiteracy taunted him.

Hearing of his death knocked the heart out of me. It was the first time someone I was acquainted with had taken their own life. For days and nights I brooded on what might have pushed him over the edge.

The River Shannon

The river Shannon is in my mind
Flowing through our town;
In the river Shannon you often find
People drown.
One of our neighbours was fished out last week
Down on Arthur's Quay.
When I heard the news I couldn't speak
And the heart sank in me.

The river Shannon is in my mind
And it's in my blood.
In the river Shannon you often find
Bodies in the mud.
A young girl was found washed up down river;
Her name was Madeline.
A boy found weeks later
Was just seventeen.

And I stood there one time not so long ago
With my reflection troubling the flow.

The river Shannon is in my mind
And it's in my soul.
The river Shannon, you often find,
Takes its toll:
A brother and sister went there, I read,
Left a note on their door:
"Gone to the river for good", the note read.
They didn't go home anymore.

At an early age I discovered that one of the surest ways of overcoming life's heaviness or gravity was through romantic love. There's no mystery in this, for what basically happens is that the awe-struck lover simply forgets himself in the company of the beloved, and in forgetting himself he automatically off-loads the heavy weight of a self-centred existence.

I first learned something of this with Margaret Close at the first dance I attended. It was a ceili in the *Jes* hall and I didn't know the first thing about Irish dancing. When I spotted Margaret - a pretty little blue-eyed blonde - doing a jig with a gangly boy who kept tripping over her, I observed how patient she was being and decided that she was the partner for me.

By a stroke of luck, when I asked her "up" the band broke into a slow waltz. Noticing the awkwardness of my opening steps Margaret gave me a few pointers on foot control. After that it was like steering dodgems at a carnival. The slight pressure of her small breasts against my chest put zest in my step, but I was too shy to start a conversation. Eventually Margaret broke the ice by commenting on the fancy necktie I was wearing (one I had filched from my father's vast collection) which had the profile of an eagle on the front with a red rhinestone eye. Margaret thought the bird was a hawk. I put her straight and informed her that the eyesight of eagles is nine times greater than that of humans. This piece of general knowledge impressed her so much she tightened her grip on my hip and told me her name. Making a joke of her surname I pressed closer to her and smiled.

We spent the rest of the night dancing together and at the end of the dance she let me walk her home. Half way across the city, I discovered that Margaret lived in one of the roughest parts of Limerick. Apologising for taking me so far out of my way, she suggested that I turn back, admitting that her neighbourhood was a no-go zone after dark. I put on a brave face, lied that I wasn't afraid, and insisted on walking her to her door. It was a risky thing to do, but I was well rewarded.

Margaret

Love is a delicate thing
When it first comes round;
Think of gentle wings
Above hard ground;
When I met Margaret time started to fly
In the sky-blue of her eye.

She lived in a poor part of town
In a bleak estate;
The neighbourhood was run-down
But when we kissed at her gate
My heart started beating like a bird leaving a nest;
 I could feel wings inside my chest.

Then I rose above the town;
Gravity couldn't keep me down;
All my weight fell away
And I began to gasp and I began to sway.
The schools, the factories and the bars
 I was above them seeing stars;
 It really took my breath away –
 The rising up and then the Milky Way.

Love is featherbrained
When it first comes;
It won't be tied or chained
Down by sums;
Though I knew Margaret was two years older than me,
I didn't tell her I was younger than she.

I just rose above the town;
Gravity couldn't keep me down.

It's strange the tricks our memories can play on us. For years I lived under the misapprehension that Margaret jilted me because of our age difference, but soon after I released her song on the first edition of **Just Another Town** I received a letter from her from London - where she now lives, more than forty years after the event - with an enclosed copy of a page from her 1964 Diary with this entry:

> ...I had a date to meet this fella that I met at a ceili but he never showed up...

The fallibility of memory!

I often wonder what my life might have been like had I married a local girl and settled down in the hometown. Observing the quiet existence of young married couples while I was growing up, I was conscious that most women – including my own mother – got the raw end of the stick in the marriage contract, at a time when it was frowned on for women to work outside the home.

Young Mothers

Young mothers standing by their front-doors
Resting from their daily chores;
On their feet, their eyes are straying
Around a street where children are playing;
They often greet a neighbour saying,
"It's another cloudy day"

Young mothers talking among themselves
Between cooking meals and dusting shelves.
Then they hear a baby crying; somewhere near
The sound is flying to the ear
Of the one sighing
In another cloudy day.

And their beauty is fading,
'Cause the worries of life
Have wrinkles invading
The face of a wife.

Young mothers waiting outside schools
For bright children and little fools;
They watch them run in little races;
Watch their fun with smiling faces
While the sun comes out in places
In another cloudy day.

A gang of us were chopping down sally trees on the banks of the Shannon for the May bonfire when one of the older boys, Billy R – a nasty creature, if ever there was one - made a snide remark about my mother. "Where's your mammy, Duhan? In hospital again, is she? What's she in for this time, huh?"

I hadn't a clue what he was getting at but the twitching grin on his face irked the hell out of me. "What's it to you, rat-face?" Grinding his teeth, Billy came over and snatched the hatchet from my hand and threw it way out into the mudflats, close to the river where I hadn't a hope of retrieving it. Grabbing another hatchet from one of the boys working with me, I flew at Billy with blade held high but two of the older boys restrained me before I reached my target. Though the gang spent an hour or so trying to locate the lost hatchet by creating a walkway out over the mud with the felled trees, we had to concede defeat in the end.

While we were dragging the muddy trees back to our neighbourhood I tried to think up some feasible excuse to tell my father about the missing hatchet. I dreaded going home and the nearer we drew to our street the deeper the dread grew.

When we eventually arrived at the avenue where we stored the trees, Billy started taunting me again, only this time he was more direct. "Were you ever in the nuthouse, Duhan? I heard my mother saying that your mother has been up there a few times. Is it true she's mad?" I dived at Billy and tore at his face with murderous intent. Within seconds he was streaming blood. A couple of men from the neighbourhood broke up the fight and one of them marched me by the scruff of the neck to our house and told my father of the incident, blaming me as the chief culprit. Still panting like a wild animal, I explained to my father what Billy had done with our hatchet and then I broke into tears and told him what he had said about my mother. My father's face grew rigid with anger. He ordered the man who was still holding me by the neck to let me go and then he told me to go back and give Billy another few thumps for him.

Having been orphaned out to a blind relative when
she was just four years of age, following the death of
her mother and the loss of her bereft father to drink,
my mother was frail by nature. Fate struck again in her
early marriage when her first son died on the same day
that my paternal grandfather passed away, after my
mother had nursed them both for six months while my
father was away at sea. That's when she had her first
breakdown. In those days we only had one hurtful
word for it.

Everything will be Alright

Sister, we're alone in the middle of the night
Counting car-lights on the ceiling,
Everything will be alright.
Mother had a breakdown, that's 'cause she was sad,
Let's just count the car lights;
Mother isn't mad.

Mother isn't mad, she's just sad;
Mother isn't mad, I tell you, and father isn't bad.

Sister, stop your crying, why can't you play the game:
The lights coming from the left are yours,
The ones from the right I claim.
Sister, stop your crying, all old people are the same;
It happens to them all, Bobby told me
His mother's just the same.

Mother isn't mad, she's just sad;
Mother isn't mad, I tell you, and father isn't bad

A Winter's Night ends **Just Another Town** on the high note of a boy gripped in a breathtaking experience that "threw light on everything" for him. The light he is singing about isn't just the natural light illuminated by the angelic wing of moon he is observing in the night sky above his hometown but is an inner light that informs him that the surrounding darkness and pain of the world – including, maybe, the darkness and pain of some of the songs on **Just Another Town** itself - somehow dissolve in God's pure purpose.

 The experience related to in the lyric was influenced by the New Testament story of the shepherds' visitation from the heavenly host at Advent but it is also grounded in a real life experience I had on a frosty evening when I was no more than five or six years of age. The memory is so old and so pure I found I could only sing it from a third person perspective.

I was standing in the cold street looking up over
the rooftops and out into the universe where a million
stars were glittering like hoarfrost on the tops
of the cars along the road, and I remember feeling
that the vast stretch of the Milky Way was just a
ceiling to our town and that all the houses along
the street with their yellow windows and smoking
chimney-pots were rooms in the great house of the town,
and that all the people in them were one close family.

A Winter's Night

Winter was the season
In the chilly street
When a young boy among children
Unsteady on his feet
Looked above the rooftops
Where in the sky
A million stars like hoarfrost
Twinkled in his eye,

And the moon, like an angel,
Spread its opal wing
Above those chosen children
And threw light on everything,
Threw light on everything.

Warm was the feeling
In the young boy's soul
While the other children
Shivered in the cold
Till the young boy told them
Of the wondrous sight,
Then all together
They looked up into the night,

Where the moon, like an angel,
Spread its opal wing
Above those chosen children
And threw light on everything,
Threw light on everything.

Introduction to Chapter Two

To the Light charts my years on the road with bands in the sixties and seventies, tilting for fame and the girl. Its tone & rhythm come from the radios, jukeboxes, cafes, bars, dancehalls and nightclubs of the time it sings of. It is not a success story; numerous failures and heartaches are encountered on the road.

One of a score of managers who quit working with me out of a sense of frustration - Terry O'Neill - told me that I was the only person he'd encountered in a long career in the music business with "a will to fail". This isn't quite true. But my uncompromising attitude to my work down the years has no doubt contributed to keeping success from my door.

Though I never quite make "the big time" in these pages, I eventually find the girl and experience a moment of transcendence that convinces me of the truth of a newspaper quotation that I once jotted into my song journal: "We Irish are suspicious of success knowing that there is a lot more of the infinite in its opposite."

Chapter Two

To The Light

And the heavens were all aglow
shedding light on all below
and I felt the world turning
journeying
in the sea of night
and my heart started burning
for our returning to the light

Just Another Town ends on the bright note of me as a boy gazing up at the stars in a state of mystical wonderment. **To The Light** begins with me as a starry-eyed youth heading out on the road with my head full of high intentions.

Maybe it was purely coincidental but, after four or five years on the road going nowhere, I happened upon a dog-eared copy of the novel Don Quixote in a second-hand Dublin bookshop on the week my first band broke up. Reading about the mad knight's wayward life in knight-chivalry was so like my bewildered career in the music business, I decided to use Don's story as a framework to describe my own life on the road.

Though altruistic by nature, Don Quixote's main aim was to make the big time as a knight in shining armour so as to win the love of his lady in waiting, Dulcinea, who was a figment of his imagination.

For most of my early career I too lived under the dotty illusion of aiming for the stars so as to impress the girl of my dreams - a nebulous creature I hadn't met yet but one that I felt sure was waiting around every corner.

Don Quixote

I'm Don Quixote, I'm on the road again;
My band's called Sancho, we're on the move again;
My horsepower now is in a transit van;
My lance has strings, I'm a music man.

For years I listened to the radio;
Each night I'd tune in to the music show.
I'd sing along with all the songs I knew;
They helped me bear the darkness as it grew.

My eyes were on the stars, though distant and far,
I followed in their course searching for the source
Of energy and light to illuminate the night
And make my dreams bright.

Then the wild thought took a hold of me
That the bright dream was reality
And so began the story
Of my quest for love through glory.

When I was twelve or thirteen I witnessed a boy of roughly the same age as myself singing Blue Suede Shoes in a local hall and the huge round of applause he drew from the crowd filled me with such envy I later entered a carnival talent contest with my pal Cha Haran, to see if we could achieve the same kind of adulation. Because there was no backing band, we mimed Rave On to Buddy Holly's recording playing in the background. Despite the fact that my Elvis gyrations caused the record to skip a few times, the crowd loved us and we were awarded second prize by the panel of adjudicators. While we were picking up our award, however, the parish priest - and chairman of the contest's organising committee - objected to our win on the grounds that popular culture like ours was "leading a whole generation astray". So Cha and I had to swallow our pride (a pride already dented by having conceded first prize to a ventriloquist) and hand back the runner-up award of two hundred Sweet Afton cigarettes to the MC before slinking off the stage with burning faces.

Despite this aborted win, the stage-bug was firmly planted and before I was fifteen I was on the road with my first band, The Intentions, later Granny's Intentions (most of whom now are grandads).

Our first misadventure on the road came when we teamed up with Dublin manager, Mike D (an ex advertising executive who claimed to have penned the famous biscuit slogan "How do they get the figs in the Fig Roll?"). Mike booked us into a two week residency in a club in Germany that went bankrupt on the eve of our departure, spoiling our dream of following the Beatles to instant stardom. Having broken our parents' hearts by turning pro, there was no turning back.

Against Mike's advice, we moved into his flat in Leeson Street (which had become a squat since he'd quit his PR job after being cheated out of credit for the biscuit ad) and there we lived on our wits and hand-outs from Mike's soft-hearted mistress, Jacinta. For four or five weeks the six of us – Hoggy, Jack, Guido, Cha, John and I – bedded down on a grimy floor with a couple of grubby blankets, sleeping as much as fourteen hours a day to ward off the cold and hunger pangs. On a lucky night, Jacinta would throw us a few bags of chips on her way home from her night shift and occasionally we'd find a smoked cod in one of the greasy bags. Jacinta was our saviour. During the second week of accepting her charity we discovered that she was a lady of the night. But this only bolstered our respect for her, for by then we had also learned that most of her earnings went on supporting her family in a Dublin council estate.

Jacinta adored "Mikey" and was forever buying him expensive presents. What she didn't know was that Mike had another girl out in middle-class suburbia. Mike was a bag of contradictions. One day he'd be up in the air, concocting all sorts of grandiose plans for the band's future, the next, down in the dumps, unable to get out of bed. Big into séances, he contacted a spirit from the other world on his Ouija board one night who spelled out for him that the band would never "hit the big time". He lost interest in us after that. Eventually we sacked him and found a new place to live. That was the last we saw of Jacinta, though we later learned that Mike had left her to marry his middle-class alternative.

My sympathies lie with the unfortunates
of this world who want to live on a higher
plane than the flat level of ordinary existence
but often end up lowest of all.

My Gravity

I sing for the lonely souls
Who haunt this world with unearthly goals;
In the streets of every town
See them daily coming down,
See them daily coming down.

I sing for the lovers, the drunks,
Whose high aim like that of monks
Is to rise above the weight
Of man's heavy earthly state,
Of man's heavy earthly state.

But most of all I sing to be free
Of a heavy heart in me – my gravity.

I sing for those driven insane
By the weight of the strain
Of holding up beneath the press
Of a world under stress,
Of a world under stress.

I sing for the lonely souls
Who haunt this world with unearthly goals.
In the streets of every town
See them daily coming down,
See *us* daily coming down.

At a party close to the flat in Dun Laoghaire where the band moved, I rescued a young convent girl, Mary, from a groping drunk and walked her home. Beneath the creaking boughs of an oak tree across from a three story Georgian house where Mary said her parents would be waiting up for her, we kissed and made a date to walk the prom the following night. For weeks we went out together and ended each date beneath the oak boughs.

After our fifth or sixth tryst, while I was walking away from the tree with my eyes on the stars, I realised that the next date I'd arranged with Mary clashed with one of the band's bookings so I hurried back to make different arrangements. As I approached the big house I was surprised to see Mary turning away from the front gate and walking past a line of neighbouring houses. When she came to the end of the row she turned into a shadowy lane. Curious to know where she was going so late, I followed her at a distance. After trailing through several dark alleys I came to what seemed a council estate of small semis with tiny front gardens. Mary entered one of these with a key she took from her handbag. Puzzled, I waited till the following night to get to the bottom of the mystery.

After our twenty minute fling beneath the boughs on this occasion, Mary walked as usual towards the front gate of the big house and, as soon as she thought I was out of sight, veered left and followed the same route she'd taken the night before, with me close on her heels. This time when she went to insert her key in the front door of the semi, I stepped from the shadows and asked her what she was up to. Startled, she hummed and hawed and then broke down and admitted that the council house was her real home and not the mini mansion across from the oak. When I asked her why she'd invented such a lie she told me that most of her friends lived in big houses and confessed that she was ashamed of the small house we were standing outside.

I continued going out with Mary till the band moved to London, then we lost contact. I tried to write a song for her years later but all I managed was a single verse.

Like frightened thieves
we fumbled at the lock
of stolen treasure
in the shadow of sighing boughs
but ran in fear of the pleasure.

With an ambitious new manager, we moved to London and luck seemed on our side. Within months we were signed to the prestigious Deram Record Label and released our first single.

The Story of David – a self-penned tale of a would-be poet who throws up a clerical job for his art but ends up on the dole – was released to a fanfare of positive reviews, but the ominous tone of failure in the lyric didn't help its chances: *If you're stuck you'd better give up/And go back to work, David Miller.* Though tipped for the top, the record bombed in England but was a minor hit in Ireland, which gave us the opportunity to return home in some glory for a national tour.

During this trip I met Helen in a Dublin beat-club and everything went topsy-turvy.

A young Bette Davis look-alike in a polka-dot dress, Helen had an intellectual ingredient in her makeup that I found irresistible. She took me to art galleries and museums and gave me the first book I ever read, Franz Kafka's *The Castle*. By the time I finished reading the novel I was a convert to literature. I was also in love (or at least I thought I was). The only problem was that the band's Irish tour ended soon after I met Helen so I was back in London before I knew it, nursing an aching heart.

> On lonely summer days I will be thinking of you,
> my daydreams will keep me from sorrow,
> and hope you'll send a sheet of sadness when I am gone.

Helen did write to me during the next few months but most of her letters were mere lists of poetry books and novels.

After another flop single, Deram Records put pressure on the band to record a commercial song called Never An Everyday Thing. Another band released the same number soon after us and the divided airplay kept both versions well outside the British top twenty. Back in Ireland, however, we had another hit, which drew us home for another tour. This gave me the opportunity to take up where I'd left off with Helen.

On an evening stroll through the back streets and lanes of South Dublin, Helen and I took shelter from a shower in an abandoned derelict house. Downstairs was damp and covered in cobwebs and dust, so we climbed a rotting stairway and entered a dry, musty room with a low ceiling. Picture shapes and furniture markings were visible on the faded walls but the room was empty except for some shelving beside a small window. On one of the shelves, Helen found two dusty black and white photographs, one of a couple dressed in stiff clothes of the fifties (a wedding snap, judging by the neat outfits and intimate pose of the pair), the other of an infant in what looked like a baptismal gown. While we were poring, head to head, over these old snaps – speculating on whether the young couple were the child's parents – I noticed the ghosted imprint of a bed-headboard on the wall we were standing by with oily head stains on the faded floral wallpaper above it. Spotting this at the same time as me, Helen smiled and lowered her eyes. I took off my jacket and spread it on the dusty floor where the bed had once been and we lay on it and started kissing. The floorboards beneath us creaked. We broke away from one another's lips and Helen laughed. I looked into her eyes. Her irises were dilating and contracting like exotic sea creatures. I leaned down and kissed a network of fine blue veins pulsating at the side of her eye. Helen smiled, nervously. I slipped my hand between her legs. She jerked and stopped my hand from moving upward.

I lacked confidence in speaking until I started writing song lyrics. The discovery that I could explain myself clearly by ordering words on a page was a revelation.

We Both Need to Know

I want to try and say all that I have to say
For it's the only way you'll know about me.
You need some time to think on things that I say;
I need to know the truth about you and me.

Nothing can go right till I see if you'll be my bride,
My songs are my guide.

You're my comfort and delight
I'm haunted with thoughts of you at night,
O please become my cheering light
And make things bright.

When I got up the courage to sing We Both Need to Know to Helen she was completely taken aback by the intensity of my feelings. Noticing that I had rifled a few of the rhymes from a translation of Brian Merriman's *The Midnight Court* (which she herself had given me), she taunted me for being a plagiarist, but this was just a smokescreen to cover up the shock of being overwhelmed by my juvenile proposition.

A few nights after I sang the song to her, Helen and I came upon a tramp who peddled his life-story to us before panhandling me for small change. On the same night Helen and I had a flaming row which ended in Helen stalking off in a huff, setting a pattern that repeated itself again and again during the following weeks and ended finally on a rainy night while the wind was appropriately howling.

The Beggar

Do you remember the old tramp
We met while going to a party?
His face was lit by a street-lamp,
He told us his life-story:
Told us all about the wife he'd had
When he was much younger:
When she died it nearly drove him mad
'Cause he really loved her.

Do you remember the look in his eye
As he told us about her?
Almost twenty years had gone by
Yet he hadn't forgotten her.
After they buried her he couldn't adjust
To life on his own;
That's when he got the wanderlust,
Became a rolling stone.

Do you remember the way you laughed
After I gave the tramp silver?
You told me that I was daft
To believe such a beggar.
Two weeks later I was begging you
Not to walk out on me
But you went and you put me through
The worst pain I've ever had.

Pleading with a departing lover who has clearly made up their mind to leave must be one of the most counterproductive moves a jilted man can make, yet we do it. On the night Helen ditched me I drank myself silly and went for a staggering walk in a deluge.

The Night You Left Me

The whiskey didn't kill the pain
So I walked and walked in the rain
Through dark streets and lanes
The night you left me.

My thoughts were as black as the sky.
I turned from each passer-by,
Had so much rain in my eye
The night you left me.

With nowhere to go, in my despair,
I went so low going nowhere.

The whiskey didn't help at all;
In fact it even made me fall,
I needed the support of the wall
The night you left me.

One of the worst things about being jilted is that it makes you feel inadequate. In an effort to get to the bottom of my rejection, I plumbed the history of the doomed relationship for possible fault lines and came up with verses like this:

Helen's Mother

The week before she left me
Helen introduced me to her mother –
Lower middle class
But high ambitions for her daughter.
When we sat down to tea
Mummy got her knife into position,
Cut the apple-tart
And opened an inquisition:
She said, "It must be a thrill, your profession,
But is it profitable singing for a living?
They say it's insecure living on song,
So if you should end up poor
Have you anything to fall back on?"

If the timing of this last supper was significant, then the location Helen chose to break the bad news to me seemed even more relevant.

Our Last Drive

On the night you said you were leaving me
We took a final drive through the city.
You were at the wheel; you were in control,
Took the course you chose without pity.

Was it by coincidence that we ended up
In a part of town so bleak and rough
Where the poor live in poverty,
Was there a lesson there to be learned by me?
Was it just by chance that you drove me there
At a time when my career was going nowhere?
Did you take me there so that I could see
The type of place you thought you'd end up living in
If you stayed with me?

It was raining hard as we drove along,
As you told me your love was dying.
I felt so much pain I could hardly talk
While the windscreen was crying.

The ending of my relationship with Helen couldn't have come at a worse time. After the band's six or seven week Irish tour – playing at higher fees than we'd ever gone out for - our manager held back most of the profits against debts he claimed we'd accrued over the barren months in London during the previous year and a half. None of us could recall being bankrolled to such an extent during this period but our manager produced a sheaf of invoices and receipts as proof of his claim, and there wasn't a thing we could do about it. Our manager then handed in his resignation and went off and started his own music shop.

> We got the credit and he got the gold,
> Now we live on credit and he's rich, we're told.

Rather than return to London - where our reputation had been tarnished by our latest flop single - we moved into cheap bed-sits in Dublin and tightened our belts. A series of line-up changes in the band over the next few months depleted our spirits further and left us wondering if there was any point in going on. During this bleak period I tried to resume contact with Helen but she refused to even talk to me on the phone. Cynical and bitter, I wrote a song called Old Lover's Can't Be Friends and convinced myself that I was better off without her.

The Poker

If you had stayed with me, my fiery lover,
By now you'd be an ember in my brain,
And all my memories of you would have no power
Like ashes left out in the rain;
And still I'd go on poking you with spite until a cinder,
If you had stayed with me, my fiery lover.

While I was licking my wounds over Helen, Sue-Ann called to see me on the evening her boyfriend, Joey (a fan of the band) went into hospital to have his tonsils removed. Apprehensive about being alone in my bedsit with a good looking girl, I suggested going to a local bar for a few drinks. While knocking back some beers and chatting about Joey and my ex, I began to feel cheerful for the first time in ages and Sue-Ann seemed to be enjoying my company too. At closing time, rather than go our separate ways, we bought a bottle of Martini and continued chatting in front of the electric fire back at my place. For an hour or so we sipped vermouth and became quite tipsy while discussing Joey's and Helen's faults and failings. At one point Sue-Ann complained that Joey was a "stay-at-home stick-in-the-mud" and I in turn ran Helen down for being an "arty-farty mammy's-girl".

At midnight I made a silly remark about some freckles around Sue-Ann's nose, suggesting that they looked fake. To prove that they were real, Sue-Ann leaned forward and asked me to rub them. While I was doing this – glad to be proved wrong - I looked into her eyes and, before I knew it, found myself kissing her. When Sue-Ann showed no sign of stopping me, I took her hand and led her to my single bed where we kissed again lying outside the covers. Though she offered no resistance, she remained pretty lifeless on the bed beside me. After a few minutes, I disentangled myself from her limp embrace and made some kind of an apology while walking her to a nearby taxi rank. When I got back to my room, I breathed a sign of relief.

The following night Sue-Ann showed up at my place again, fluttering her false eyelashes, telling me that she had just come from the hospital where Joey was recuperating after a successful throat operation. Though I had felt a few pangs of guilt during the day over my betrayal of Joey, I was vaguely glad to see Sue-Ann again. Without alluding to the incident of the night before, we went to the pub and, after a few chatty beers, bought another bottle of Martini and returned to my room and had another session on my bed, outside the blankets.

In the middle of this second smooch Sue-Ann started telling me that Joey was due to get out of hospital in two days' time. Interpreting this interruption as a rebuke, I got off the bed and walked Sue-Ann to a taxi, sure that we were parting for good.

Astonishingly, she showed up again the following night (the eve of Joey's discharge) slightly later than usual but dressed to the nines as always in a tight-fitting outfit that showed off her waif-like figure to full advantage. Despite feeling puzzled and confused, I was again strangely glad to see her. Instead of going to the pub we went to an off licence and bought two bottles of Martini then returned to the flat and downed both bottles during the next few hours. On this occasion we didn't make it to my bed; we just slumped in armchairs by the fire, chatting. At around ten o'clock Sue-Ann started to tell me in a matter-of-fact kind of way that she had been to see Joey again that afternoon and had told him of her visits to my room. To allay my fears, she assured me that I had no need to worry. "Joey isn't the jealous type. In fact, he told me to tell you that he's going to call to see you when he gets out of hospital."

Alarmed, I got to my feet and started to light a cigarette from the electric fire. Before I managed to get it lighting there was a knock at the door and, while I was going to open it, the door came crashing in. Joey stood before me with a distorted look on his face. Glancing at Sue-Ann, he gave her a withering look and then turned to me and started cursing and calling me a traitor. Sue-Ann tried to diffuse the situation by asking Joey what he was doing out of hospital a day before his official discharge. Joey smirked and said that he had discharged himself after hearing about our "rendezvous".

With Joey fuming in front of me and Sue-Ann twisting her hands, I racked my brain for something plausible to say but, before I managed to get a word out, Joey punched me in the face several times, flooring me.

While I was attempting to get to my feet he grabbed a clump of my hair and pummelled me back onto the floor, where he launched a volley of sharp kicks to my groin. For two or three minutes he pulverised me while Sue-Ann pleaded in vain with him to stop. By the time he eventually did stop I was on the verge of unconsciousness. The last thing I remember before passing out was seeing Joey's blurred image hovering by the doorway, beckoning to Sue-Ann, who was standing above me with a look of sympathy on her mascara-smudged face. Just before my eyes clamped shut, Sue-Ann wavered for a moment, then fluttered her false eyelashes and followed Joey out the door.

We live in danger,
in danger constantly,
not just from one another,
we ourselves our own enemy.

This verse came to me in my sleep one night. I crawled out of bed at four in the morning and sang it into a tape-recorder, thinking I might expand it into a full song later. It didn't work.

When I was asked once how many hours a day I work at my craft, I explained that my working day never really ends.

The band's record producer was impressed enough by some of our new songs, he commissioned us to record a full album. Though poorly produced, **Honest Injun** came in for some favourable reviews in both the British and Irish music press when it went on general release. But once again our record company skimped on promotion, which resulted in yet another flop.

Listening back to the album years later I was disappointed to find that not one of the tracks I'd written for Helen had stood the test of time, so I had one last stab at coming up with a real song for her (at least I thought it was my last at the time of composition), concentrating on my own narcissistic motives in the affair.

There is a Girl

There is a girl I loved years ago,
She calls on me every night;
When she visits my dream she's smiling
But it doesn't seem right,
'Cause many years ago when my heart was ripe
She left it alone to wither,
Said I wasn't her type.

Still every night when the light goes out
She's waiting there for me
And like a fool I run to her,
There's something I've got to see.

In my dream I always end up
Repairing a run-down room;
It's the run-down room where she left me,
I am that room.
She stands over by the window while I make repairs;
She smiles over at my progress
And like a fool I care.

Still every night when the light goes out
She's waiting there for me
And like a fool I run to her -
There's something I've got to see.

In another dream I'm wearing
A blouse she used to wear
But when I look into the mirror
It's her face that's there.
I stand there but it's she staring back at me.
Is she really just who I wanted
To be?

One of the saddest and funniest moments in the novel *Don Quixote* occurs when the bewildered Knight, after accomplishing many of his most infamous feats - tackling windmills, routing an "army" of sheep, and freeing a chain-gang of state prisoners – decides to send his squire back to inform Dulcinea of all the great deeds he has done out in the world. By this stage Sancho has begun to twig that his master isn't the full shilling, so, rather than make the long journey home on a fool's errand, he spots a not-so-pretty looking wench coming along the dusty road on the back of a donkey and pretends that she is Dulcinea. As she approaches and Don gets a clear view of her many blemishes, he protests that his squire must be mistaken. But there's a lot at stake here for Sancho (a day-long journey over rugged terrain in broiling heat) so he insists that the rustic lass is in fact the fair lady. After a turbulent inner battle, the fanciful side of Don's brain kicks in and comes up with what for him is the only logical explanation for what has happened: Dulcinea has been transformed by some malevolent witch or sorcerer into this travesty on the donkey. But though he completely convinces himself of the truth of this harebrained notion, he still can't face meeting her until he can track down the evil witch responsible for the transformation and secure a formula to undo the spell.

I too had a similar moment of romantic disillusionment in my life (who hasn't?) when Helen tried to come back into my life ten years after she ditched me. But the old adage is true: "Beware of youthful dreams for they may be fulfilled in middle age".

When she jilted me Helen was literally in a knee-length school uniform with white blouse buttoned up to her chin. When she returned, her cleavage was on ample display and she was dressed in skimpy leather to her thighs. The animal side of my nature was aroused but my spiritual side felt let down. The problem wasn't Helen's; it was mine. "If you exalt the object of your love until your picture is a false one," wrote Fr Gerard Vann, "and if you project on them your own ideal self, then you are loving not a real person but a dream."

There is a Time

There is a time in life, it seems,
For believing in dreams,
For me it's gone.
And though I realise today
Dreams are empty anyway
I still feel wrong.

I felt cheated when you went away
But not as defeated as I felt the day
You came back and we found so little to say.

There is a time in life, I know,
When we all must outgrow
Our young ideals;
But the wisdom that we gain
Is paid for with the pain
I now feel.

I felt cheated when you went away
But not as defeated as I felt the day
You came back and we found so little to say.

There is a time in life, it seems,
For believing in dreams,
For me it's gone.

One night after I sang There is a Time on stage – introducing it as "my ode to disillusionment" - I made a very unorthodox comment on the '60s off the top of my head that set the cat among the pigeons. "I knew this guy once who had to be constrained with heavy medication and institutionalised after he went hysterical in the throes of a nervous breakdown, but back in the sixties when many of my generation went hysterically off the rails on LSD and other nefarious substances, we were patted on the back and told to get on with it."

As you might imagine, there was a long, tense silence in the club after I said this (the place being full of long-haired '60s veterans like myself) before one brave soul burst out laughing and gave the rest of the crowd license to follow suit.

Despite my refusal to look back at the '60s through rose tinted lenses (the type rock stars wear even at night) I still came up with this twist in the tale:

Fool's Review

I sometimes look back at the fool I was when I was young;
laugh when I think of me at seventeen;
blush when I think of all the silly things I've done -
but that boy stands proudly in my memory
naming fools of those who were then as I am now.

At one of the band's leanest periods in London, I became friendly with a German "escort", Frieda, who lived with her child in the room next to one I was sharing with the band's guitarist. A few days after we moved into the building a friend of Frieda's came banging on our door in a state of desperation, telling us that she had just found Frieda comatose beside her child's cot with a suicide note written to her absconded boyfriend lying beside an empty vial of sleeping tablets. After we phoned for an ambulance I helped get Frieda to her feet and forced some coffee into her. Maybe that's why she became friendly with me when she got out of hospital.

After she went back to work at her Soho nightclub, Frieda became quite chatty whenever we met in our communal kitchen. On one occasion she gave me the history of how she had come to London from a small town near Berlin twelve years before, after having disgraced her family in a prank incident that involved her imitating Lady Godiva by riding naked down the main street on the back of a pony.

Though ten years older than me, Frieda often became quite flirtatious during our kitchen chats - especially when she'd had more than her quota of G&Ts back at the club.

One night at around two in the morning she came knocking on our door in a state bordering on hysteria, telling me that an enraged client of hers was downstairs banging on the front door with a gun, convinced that Frieda had stolen his wallet during their taxi ride from Soho. While the pounding on the door grew louder, Frieda flatly denied the theft but then, just as I was beginning to believe her, she drew a brown leather wallet from her handbag and asked me to return it to her disgruntled customer. Cowering at the idea of confronting a gunslinger, I told Frieda to throw the wallet to him from her own front window. When she returned from doing this she breathed a sigh of relief and exclaimed, "You'll never guess who that vos? - one of the Kray gang! You know, the famous hoodlum brothers. They're regular customers down at the club".

At one of my lowest points on the road to fame and fortune, I returned to my seedy Hampstead bedsit in the early hours of the morning after a one night stand with a girl I'd picked up at a gig, and, while I was lying in bed brooding on the band's uncertain future, my father came into my mind singing one of the brave songs he used to sing in Joe's Bar when I was a kid. The memory lifted my spirits and later inspired a song that has been covered by many singers, including Ronnie Drew and The Dubliners.

Before Ronnie recorded another song of mine, Always Remember, he phoned me to ask if he could change one word of the lyric - an *and* or a *but* - which gives a measure of the man's integrity and shows the respect he has for the written word.

Don't Give Up Till It's Over

Don't give up till it's over,
Don't quit, if you can;
The weight upon your shoulder
Will make you a stronger man.

Grasp your nettle tightly,
Though it will burn,
Treat your failures lightly
Your luck is bound to turn.

And don't give up till it's over, etc.

Look at the autumn flowers,
How they wither and fade,
But with nature's hidden powers
Next year they'll be remade.

So don't give up till it's over, etc.

Watch the full moon rising,
Like the ghost of the sun,
Dawn will be more surprising
When a new day's begun.

My mother once told me that her grandmother literally picked her grandfather from the gutters of Limerick as a drunken soldier and knocked him into such good shape he ended up a sergeant major in the Irish army. Joan, a young school teacher with luminous eyes and a stunning figure whom I met at one of the band's final gigs, did something similar for me.

I knew that the light in your eyes had a
pure source, so when bells started ringing
after Sunday breakfast I wasn't surprised
when you hurried for mass,
for the parables and psalms,
for the sacraments.

> I took her hand and led her out into the blue
> foaming water till we were in way above our waists.
> A wave came hurtling towards us. Joan gasped
> and her tanned breasts started heaving above
> her blue bikini top. "I've never been in this deep.
> I'm frightened." I lowered my hands to her hips
> and kissed her neck. "I warned you when you teamed
> up with me that you were getting in over your head."

Joan and I spent a long hot summer camping and busking around the south of Ireland. After the vacation, we found a flat together and I buckled down to writing songs and eking out a living on the folk circuit.

After several months of scraping by, I was offered a job as lead singer with a London band, St James's Gate, who were on the cusp of signing an international recording deal for oodles of money. Though I didn't like the style of music the band played (old style rock'n'roll) or the amount of rehearsal time they spent in the pub living up to their name, I teamed up with them on the understanding that I would sing mainly my own songs.

While we were waiting for the big deal to be finalised, I moved into a tatty attic bed-sit in Chiswick. Joan joined me some time later, after throwing up her teaching job in Dublin and the pension that went with it.

The Room

The room was shabby and it was bare
But when you came and joined me there,
You turned it into home, didn't you, Joan?
You made me a home when I was alone.

The walls were peeling, the ceiling was low,
But with you there it didn't seem so;
With you it became home, didn't it, Joan?
You made me a home when I was alone.

The single bed in the corner so small and old
Could be so cold,
But after you moved in there with me
I had you to warm and hold me.

The broken glass of the window pane
Let in a summer scent when you came
And you, you built me a home, didn't you, Joan?
You made me a home when I was alone.

The move to Britain transformed Joan. She had always been bright and bubbly but in London she opened up like a summer rose. Discarding her loose tie-dyed hippy garb, she started dressing in the latest vivid tight-fitting Chelsea fashions.

One balmy night after we'd had a few drinks in a local lounge, she threw her arms around me on Chiswick's busy main street and kissed me openly in front of a stream of passersby. With my hands gripping her slim waist, I told her that she was like a tightrope walker working without a safety net for the first time, suggesting that the net in question was the net income she'd thrown up to be with me. She laughed at the idea and joked that the only reason she'd joined me was for the excitement of the rock-star lifestyle (poor girl, if only she knew).

When we arrived at our attic bedsit there was a strong smell of apples and roses coming through the broken window, which we'd opened earlier to clear out a gas-stench from a leaking pipe. Leaning over the sill, Joan breathed in the scented air rising from the neighbouring gardens and said that the smell reminded her of the countryside around her parents' farm in county Galway at harvest time.

I joined her at the window and looked into her eyes. Her mouth opened and a prominent incisor that she was in the habit of concealing with her upper lip became visible. I touched it. She smiled and the tooth became even more exposed. I ran the back of my hand over her cheek and asked her if she had any regrets about moving to London. She smiled and started taking off her dress while singing an old song of mine, We Both Need To Know. I laughed at her tuneless voice and reminded her that the song she was singing was written for another girl. She shrugged and slipped into our single bed, telling me that she didn't care. I started getting undressed, turning away to hide my growing desire. Joan smiled and told me to turn around. I turned and stared into her gleaming eyes. She smiled shyly and moved in in the bed. I stepped towards her, breathing in the rose scented air, telling her that some day I would write her a far far better song.

When my first flame died
and you became my love,
a fresh breath of air
made sparks appear,
and my heart, like coal,
lit up and my soul took fire,
while out in your bed
you grew blushing red
my flower.

While the romantic side of my life was thriving, my position in St James's Gate didn't work out at all to my satisfaction. After I refused to sing several limp songs that they presented me with for our first recording session, tensions mounted. The band had hired in an Italian/American producer for the recordings, Steve V, who ended up favouring my songs over the other writers in the band. This created deep rivalry in the camp and gave me a puffed up feeling that I could go it alone if the band failed. On the eve of the band signing the dotted line with the record company I had a flaring row with the group's leader which resulted in me leaving the band. I later went on to record a solo album with Steve V, but at this juncture, instead of moving from our Chiswick bed-sit to a pad on the Chelsea High Road - as Joan and I were planning to do - we ended up relocating to the old bog road in County Galway where Joan's parents ran a small farm.

I'd spent half my life dreaming with my eyes on the stars,
so when we moved to the farm I had a rude awakening:
a donkey brayed in a far field, a cow lowed in a paddock,
a pig grunted to its farrow, a cock crowed on a dung-
heap. Out on the ploughed land among the scarecrows
with my hands in the dirt, I hankered for the easy
life on the open road. O yes, a rude awakening brought
me down to earth with a bang. But after this hard planting,
I'll be laughing, reaping.

I'm Lucky I Had You

When we moved to the country
After the deal fell through
It wasn't easy for a city boy like me
I'm lucky I had you.

I knew so little of farming,
When I tried the little I knew
I went so low when the crop didn't grow,
I'm lucky I had you.

I'm lucky I had you, love,
Lucky I had you;
When everything fell through, love,
You knew what to do
And your love pulled us through.

When autumn turned to winter,
When there was so little to do,
Deep in the throes of the frost and snows
I'm lucky I had you.

The farm-work outlined in I'm Lucky I Had You is some-what exaggerated, but I did try my hand at kitchen gardening while I was living on Joan's parents' farm. In a fenced-off plot allocated to me by Joan's father, Denny, I planted a wide range of vegetables, and not just your common or garden fare of potatoes, cabbage, turnnips parsnips, onion, carrots and other local pro-duce. As well as red and green peppers, broccoli, aubergines and courgettes, I sowed a variety of uncommon lettuces, cucumbers, and, my most ambitious seedling of all, corn on the cob.

While I was planting these exotic varieties, several locals came by scoffing at my ambitious beds, predicting that my foreign plants wouldn't grow. But they were wrong. By mid June my plot was dense with green verdure, and while Joan informed me that most of this was weed, some of my plants were beginning to show signs of life beneath the wild entanglements. To fight off the vetch, nettles, thistles and thorns, I battled each day with my hoe and rake, dripping with sweat in the summer heat but enjoying the toil none the less. At the beginning of July, Joan's sister, Carmel, gave me an unorthodox gardening book, *Help Your Plants Grow with Music*, which astonishingly suggested that certain kinds of plant life thrive on music and song. Sceptical as I am about such outlandish esoteric claims, I took my guitar out to the garden early one morning before the locals were up and tested the theory on my peppers and corn with a couple of my more gentle and melodic ballads. I can't say for certain that my songs had the desired effect but by mid-July the corn stalks were up to my waist and the beaded cobs were beginning to form at the heart of the spreading ears. I was on a high from then on, waiting in anticipation for harvest time. During the final week of July I composed a verse in honour of my garden called Lover:

> I placed my fingers in your crumpled bed,
> spilled my seed in your dark crevices
> and waited for the wet spring and the hot summer.

In the second week of August a lean herd of cattle from one of the neighbouring farms - owned by one of the most miserly farmers in the locality, who deliberately forced his cattle onto the *long acre* for free grazing - got a whiff of my broccoli and lettuce and broke into my garden in the dead of night, scavenging everything that they didn't trample underfoot. Had the fencing around Denny's plot been made of sturdier stuff than bits of twine, old rope, nylon tights and elastic from old knickers, it might have kept the hungry beasts at bay. As it was they had a field day, sending me into a dark depression when I discovered the devastated plot.

During the darkening months of autumn - after I got over the loss of my harvest - I reworked some old songs and sent them to record companies in London in the hope of getting a new recording deal, but all my demos came back with rejection slips that sent me into a further downward spiral of despair. As we entered the black tunnel of winter I began to develop a range of psychosomatic ailments - ulcers, allergies, headaches and, the biggest pain in the arse of all, haemorrhoids. To avoid negative thinking, I started writing an autobiographical account of my early years of growing up in Limerick, in the style of Joyce's *Portrait of the Artist as a Young Man*, but without Joyce's prose talent. Though my rambling and confused hand-written manuscript eventually meandered into the sand, some of the early events I unearthed began to re-emerge as songs.

> It was the clear memory of the spirited boy
> that I had been while growing up that gave
> me the confidence to attempt to mark my place
> in the world. My travails on the road to manhood
> had made me forget who I really was, and am.

During my second spring and summer on the land, I yielded a bumper crop of two dozen songs or more, including all the numbers from my **Just Another Town** album. For the first time in my career I was certain that I had found my own voice as a songwriter. This restored my self-belief and, with the strong conviction that I was finally going to make a mark with my work, I married Joan in a small chapel in the village of Bullaun on the bright sunny afternoon of 11 June 1975. At the wedding reception I entertained our guests with a selection of Hank William's love songs (we couldn't afford to hire a band) and a few of my own new upbeat numbers.

Girls In my Memory

It's funny how you remind me of
Certain girls I've loved
Who keep turning up in my dreams.
I remember one had eyes like you,
They were sky-blue
And I searched them for a sunny beam.

You keep reminding me
Of girls in my memory
And they keep reminding me of you.

It's funny now when I look at you
I see a few of the faces
That keep haunting me.
One talks like the way you talk,
Another has your walk,
Another kisses like you kiss me.

You keep reminding me
Of girls in my memory
And they keep reminding me of you.

It's funny how certain moments with you
Remind me too
Of certain moments I've lived before;
Like a night on a moonlit beach
I remember your speech
Because another girl had said it before.

You keep reminding me
Of girls in my memory
And they keep reminding me of you.

The title of another lyric I wrote at this time - I Didn't Mean To Call You Josephine, Eileen - always raised a heckle at gigs but the song itself wasn't up to scratch so I dropped it. But I've written numerous songs with girls' names as titles: Mary, Margaret, Joan and Molly, to name a few. After singing several of these at a concert in Cork some time back a girl approached me after I came off stage with a wry smile, saying: "If you don't mind me asking, how many girls have you gone out with exactly?" to which I coyly replied, "Not as many as you might think. Most of the girls' names in my titles are pseudonyms for my one-and-only who prefers to remain anonymous."

You always woke long after me, but once on a summer
morning soon after we married you woke at dawn
and asked me to go mushroom picking. We crept out of
the cottage, yawning and rubbing our eyes. Outside there
was bird-song in a pink coral sky and the misty fields
were grey with dewy spider-webs. Sheep looked up from
their early grazing, a cow lowed near the dirt-track,
a hare shot across a tussocky hillock. When we reached
the "mushroom field" we filled a red basin to the brim
with a white froth of mushrooms. Back in the cottage we
left the vessel on the kitchen table beside the milk jug
and crept back to bed and warmed one another
with our limbs.

Molly

O Molly believe me,
Please don't tease me,
You know I'm out on my own;
I've got nowhere to call home,
I'm on this planet alone.

O Molly come with me,
You know you lift me;
You know together it's nice,
I love to hear your voice,
You're my own choice.

Don't leave me just memory,
You're my only address.
Tell me you need me
And there's nobody else.

O Molly believe me,
I know you can read me,
Can't you see on my face
Doubt has replaced
The sure lines you once traced.

Don't leave me just memory,
You're my only address.
Tell me you need me
And there's nobody else.

I wrote Molly under a cloud of jealousy, suspecting that Joan had taken a shine to another man. She flatly denied the charge but did so in a way that left me in a state of animated doubt, teasing me that a certain amount of romantic uncertainty was healthy in a relationship.

Another reason she played me along, I suspect, was because at this time I was writing songs about "girls in my memory" and one of Joan's favourite aphorisms has always been, "What's sauce for the goose is sauce for the gander".

All I Need

I've been let down but now I've overcome the pain
And now I'm back here on this train,
Rolling away from disappointment and shame,
Rolling on with my old flame.

They've taken all I had but you, Love,
But you love are all I need.

For too long I sat nursing my despair,
Then I fought it like a bear.
Now I shoulder the weight of all my care
With the gentle strength of prayer.

They've taken all I had but you, Love,
But you love are all I need.

One of the finest compliments that Joan has ever paid me in relation to my work came in the form of an insult. "It never ceases to amaze me how pure and honest and open you can be in your songs, and yet, outside of them, how much of a bastard and a pain in the arse you can be at times."

As sincere as I've striven to be in my work, I'm very much aware of a calculated side to my artistic nature that is always on the hunt for applause and praise. I'm not proud of this trait, so I make light of it whenever I can with a bit of wry humour. For instance, I never leave the stage at the end of my performances and come back for encores. Instead I make a joke about how my old band used to stand in the wings at the end of our gigs (as most performing acts do) nudging one another back into the limelight before the fading applause died down altogether.

The Spider

In my room I made this melody,
It's a web for me, and I wove it well.
Up on the stage I try to catch your ear
With this song you hear, it's a spell.
When my fingers start to ply my strings
A voice begins to sing through my trap.
I do it to hear you clap;
When your hands like wings begin to flap,
Then I've got you with my songs,
You're victims, that's a fact.
My performance is full of tact;
The object of my act
Is to knock you dead,
To knock you dead!

In the spotlight above my chords
Singing for rewards, it's a lonely life.
With my stomach full of butterflies,
Waiting for applause to rise, I'm on the edge of a knife.
But when I catch you with the songs I sing,
When I begin to win my encore,
That's the buzz I adore –
Crawling back as you roar;
For then I've got you with my songs,
You're victims, that's a fact.
My performance is full of tact
For the object of my act
Is to knock you dead,
knock you DEAD.

At the end of the novel Don Quixote there's a key moment (for me) where Don's niece goes to the sick-bed of her defeated and disillusioned uncle and tries to rouse him back into action, but Don, returned to his proper senses, will have none of it, proclaiming that if he had more time in this world he would devote it to studying the Desert Fathers and sacred books.

Since I returned to practising religious faith in my early thirties (soon after I completed the final version of my Don Quixote song), I have almost burned my eyes to their sockets reading the great spiritual writers like St Paul, St Augustine, Thomas A Kempis, Thomas Aquinas, John Of The Cross, St Teresa of Avila, Pascal, Dante, George Herbert, TS Eliot, RS Lewis, Cardinal Newman, Reinhold Niebuhr, and countless others. Despite this commitment, I'm still occasionally overwhelmed with moments of doubt (my father's legacy). But for my final song of this chapter I'll leave you with a lyric inspired by an experience I had one night in a glow of bright starlight beside my soul-mate which convinced me that we are indeed voyaging towards a holy haven.

.

Before I went to bed last night I looked out
my window and saw a bright star high in the sky.
In the middle of the night I woke and again looked
out and noticed the same star much lower on the
horizon. In my half-conscious state it struck me that
the world was turning - a vehicle. I felt the motion
of the entire planet beneath me sailing through the
universe. And for an instant I felt absolutely positive
that our journey has a destination.

To the Light

I looked in the sky one night
And saw a star, clear and bright,
But so far away from me alone in the dark;
I turned from that distant light
And went to bed and slept for a while
With you by my side and woke from a dream
And looked out again –

And the heavens were all aglow,
Shedding light on all below,
And I felt the world turning,
Journeying in the sea of night,
And my heart started burning
For our returning to the light.

Yes I looked at the shining star
And was so moved by the power of light
That proved that there was fire still in my heart.
I turned to you in the dark and you woke
And your eyes caught the light of the star as we spoke
And that light in your eyes sparkled with love –

And the heavens were all aglow,
Shedding light on all below,
And I felt the world turning
Journeying in the sea of night
And my heart started burning
For our returning to the light.

Introduction to Chapter Three

The Voyage deals with family matters and family history, taking its inspiration from both the family I grew up in and the family I helped form. It is not a sentimental or nostalgic portrait but one that shows up the cracks and strains of marriage, as well as the joy of family life.

When I first released a selection of these songs on a collection called **Family Album,** my Dublin booking agent dropped me because he maintained that it was impossible to get radio and TV coverage for a product that was out of tune with the times. "The family is a dead institution," he asserted. "Find something else to sing about!"

Even Christ had reservations about the family, as verse twenty six of Luke's gospel demonstrates, where we are invoked to "hate" family members who get in the way of our following God's decrees. Despite all its shortcomings, most of us love our families and turn to them not only in times of crisis but in times of celebration as well.

Chapter Three

The Voyage

I once climbed the branches
of our old pear tree
and found some hard fruit
where none used be;
it tasted bitter,
still we all ate.

A few years back I arrived at a TV location to prerecord a duet version of The Voyage with Christy Moore, the first singer to have had a hit with it. Originally Christy and I agreed that I would sing another of my songs and he would perform The Voyage solo (he being the one who had popularised it) but a day or two before the shoot the series' producer contacted me with the news that my solo song had been dropped from the schedule due to lack of space on the programme. Disgruntled by this turn of events, I arrived on the set in a very uncertain frame of mind about singing The Voyage as a duet, for a number of reasons, but Christy tried to put my mind at rest by telling me that, after a few run-throughs, it would be "sound".

Half way into the first verse of the first run-through - while the camera crew were lining up their shots - the song collapsed due to a clash of rhythms between Christy's version and mine. I began to panic at that stage but Christy held his head, though I noticed the famous beads of sweat on his brow were beginning to swell in size. In a calm tone, he suggested trying the song again with my guitar to the fore.

After a shaky intro, Christy's guitar accompanist, Declan Sinnott, picked up on my tempo and Christy started singing the first verse in a gentle mellifluous flow, throwing me a look of approval to let me know that the arrangement was fine. As he sang the final line of verse one -"For the heart's treasures together we set sail" – he cued me to take over the relay vocal for the second verse and broke into a warm smile when I came in on time. While I was singing my opening line – "Together we're in this relationship" - I smiled back at Christy just as warmly as he had smiled at me and instantly he stopped playing and cursed into his mic: "Jayzus wept, I see what you mean, Johnny – It's like I'm Elton John and you're George Michael. Fuck that! We'd better get back to the drawing board."

The Voyage

I am a sailor and you're my first mate;
We signed on together, coupled our fate;
Hauled up our anchor, determined not to fail,
For the heart's treasure together we set sail.

With no maps to guide us we steered our own course;
Weathered the storms when the winds were gale-force;
Sat out the doldrums with patience and hope,
Working together we learned how to cope.

Life is an ocean, love is a boat,
In troubled waters it keeps us afloat.
When we started the voyage there was just me and you:
Now look around us, we have our own crew.

Together we're in this relationship;
We built it with care to last the whole trip.
Our true destination's not marked on a chart,
We're navigating for the shores of the heart.

Life is an ocean, love is a boat,
In troubled waters it keeps us afloat.
When we started the voyage there was just me and you;
Now look around us, we have our own crew.

Wallace in his Cave

A spider suspended
on a thread so thin
  I couldn't see it
clutched at my heart
and climbed thin air
right to the ceiling.

Back in the late seventies I managed to get an international recording deal with Arista Records through Mike C, a Jewish manager I teamed up with in London. With the advance I received from the company on signing the contract, Joan and I bought a house in Galway city, but, soon after we moved in with our infant son, Ronan, the record deal went belly up on the eve of the release of my first solo album. On top of this Mike became a heroin addict (he had always dabbled in drugs but the stress of losing my deal pushed him over the edge). In the middle of this turmoil I started writing a story, *The Long Enduring* (probably as a diversionary tactic to take my mind off my latest failure) partly inspired by Robert Wallace's famous moment of inspiration in defeat when he drew courage from a resilient spider. Working nine and ten hours a day on the quirky story, I drove myself into the ground and ended up almost having a nervous breakdown. While I was desperately trying to find a positive ending for my story (after my recent failures it wasn't easy) I started hearing a scratching sound in the attic above my head. At first I thought my over-stretched imagination was playing tricks on me, but then Joan heard the noise too.

We Had Our Trouble Then

There was a rat in the attic polluting our home,
It sent shivers down my backbone,
We had our trouble then, our trouble then,
We had our trouble then, Amen.

I was out of work, moping around,
Looking at the ceiling, listening for the sound,
We had our trouble then, our trouble then,
We had our trouble then, Amen.

A trap was set but the rat wouldn't bite,
I had a job to get, there was none in sight,
We had our trouble then, our trouble then,
We had our trouble then, Amen

The rat kept creeping above my head,
I was tired of sleeping and full of dread;
We had our trouble then, our trouble then,
We had our trouble then, Amen

There was a rat in the attic polluting our life,
I was worried for the kids and my wife,
We had our trouble then, our trouble then,
We had our trouble then, Amen

I lost all courage, I must confess;
I grew weak and full of distress,
We had our trouble then, our trouble then,
We had our trouble then, Amen.

There was a rat in the attic polluting my brain,
I never saw it but it caused me much pain,
We had our trouble then, hope we won't have it again.

The girl I married is typically feminine, frightened of mice – not to mind rats - but she also has a courageous side to her nature.

Some years back we were having a drink in a Galway bar with her sister Carmel when three thugs came and sat opposite us. The leader of the pack – a big burly guy with a scar under his left eye - ordered Joan to light his cigarette with the lighter lying beside her wine glass. When Joan ignored this demand the guy pulled a flick-knife from his pocket and pressed the tip of the blade to her throat. In terror, I glared at the thug wondering if I should make a grab for the knife. While I was weighing up the pros and cons, I noticed that the bulky companions were ready to pounce on me the second I made a move. During the stand-off, Joan remained as calm as a cucumber. Staring the brute straight in the eye, she smirked, as much as to say, "Go on, do it, if you have the balls!" My heart jumped to my throat. Carmel gripped my arm to restrain me. A distorted look came over the thug's face. He stared into Joan's defiant eyes for what seemed an age, then slowly he lowered the blade and backed off, cursing under his breath.

Cornerstone

You are the cornerstone of my life;
You're my backbone, lover and wife.
You make the home where I reside,
You set the tone that keeps the spirit alive.

You're the foundation of all my hope;
I am impatient, you help me cope;
Without you I'm sure I'd go astray;
You are the cure I need each day.

And in this age where marriage is dying,
I assert this commitment of mine:
Till death plays its part you have my heart,
With yours let it combine.

You are the rock on which my life is built;
You hold the stock of my courage and strength.
You are the friend on whom I'll rely
Until the end, till you or I die.

Yes, in this age where marriage is dying,
I assert this commitment of mine:
Till death plays its part, you have my heart,
With yours let it combine.

I read about this celebrity couple in a newspaper some time back (a TV host and a radio producer) who decided to "tie the knot" while maintaining their relationship on a "strictly independent basis", with each of them keeping their "own space" and putting no demands or pressures on one another after the marriage. I laughed to myself and wasn't surprised to read in the same newspaper six months later that the same couple had just separated "amicably".

After the Dance

O the warm look in your eye
When you and I met after the dance,
I saw it the other night, shining just as bright
As your first glance,
And I warmed to the sight
As I warmed on that first night years ago
When your eye held the light
Of more than the moonlight
And made the darkness glow.

Yes the brightness of that look
Held me and took me back to that moment in life
That defined for you and me a destiny
As man and wife;
And I warmed to sight
As I warmed on that first night years ago
When your eyes held the light
Of more than the moonlight
And made the darkness glow.

O the brightness of that look
Held me and took me back to that moment in time.

My parents also met at a dance. I learned this some years back when I took my aged mother for a stroll in Limerick's People's Park.

While we were taking a rest on a sunny seat near the bandstand, she filled me in on the details. To begin with, it was a triangular affair. In her late teens she was at a dance with her first steady boyfriend, Paddy T, when my father – a young sailor home from sea – breezed in looking sharper than Frank Sinatra, with oiled hair, double breasted suit and a fancy necktie. Spotting my raven-haired mother across the dance-floor, my father sauntered over, sidestepping Paddy, and asked her to dance. Sensing the chemistry between them, Paddy didn't object. Indeed, he acted so magnanimously he bows out of the song I wrote about the event after the first line (a direct quote from Paddy's lips according to my mother) so be careful or you'll miss him. But the story doesn't end there. Soon after I released the song on an album I ran into an old friend of my mother's, Mary, who, after hearing the song on the radio, filled me in on some dark details about Paddy that my mother didn't even know about.

On the day after the jilting, it seems, Mary bumped into Paddy on a street leading to the river Shannon. After telling her about the break up with my mother in a distracted and confused way, Paddy took off his wrist watch and offered it to Mary. Mary told him that a man's watch was no good to her, and Paddy walked on. Mary stood gaping after him for a few moments, then it dawned on her that he was heading for the river and she twigged his dark intent. Going after him, she used all her persuasive powers to veer him away from the desperate act. Months later, Paddy married another girl and went on to have a large family.

But that's another story. My song confines itself to those few charged moments in the dancehall when my father and mother took to the floor while the band broke into a chart hit of the day, The Band Played On.

And the Band Played

Pat said, "The best man won" and walked away.
As you turned back to John, music began to play,
And the band played "The Band Played On";
Yeah the band played "The Band Played On"
The night you chose John.

He was a young sailor whose ship had just come in;
Dancing together felt like heaven
As the band played "The Band Played On";
Yeah the band played "The Band Played On"
The night you chose John.

You were the most beautiful girl in the world,
That's what he said to you as round and round you twirled.

And now you sit with me near a bandstand in the park
And your old memory throws light on your years
                                        in the dark,
So let the band play "The Band Played On"
As the band played "The Band Played On"
The night you chose John.

I sang And the Band Played at a concert in my hometown and after my performance an elderly man approached me claiming that he was the "Pat" from my song. After confirming that he was my mother's first boyfriend he told me that, after the break-up, he had gone on to marry not once but twice. I gave him a copy of the album on which he briefly features. Before we parted, he told me that, though he had been happy in both his marriages, he had never really gotten over my mother.

If Pat's claim to two happy marriages is true, he's a lucky man, for tragedy of one kind or another seems to visit most families in the course of a lifetime.

A few years after my parents married their first son died on the same day that my father's father passed away (as already related), resulting in my mother's first breakdown. This black event haunted our house so strongly while I was growing up you could almost touch the ghost of it in the air. In my early teens I found a death certificate inscribed with my Christian name in a tin box belonging to my father. My eldest sister had told me that I had inherited my dead brother's first name but coming upon it in this faded form was a stark reminder of his living absence from our home and of my association to the vacancy.

In an intimate conversation with my father in my early teens I learned that my mother had been orphaned out to a blind relative when she was four years of age after her mother died and her bereft father turned to drink. My father believed that the instability that this trauma caused in her early life created the undertow that pulled her down when their first son died. He also blamed the inhuman way patients were treated in mental hospitals at that time for her ongoing problems later in life.

After her initial four or five month lockup period - partly in a padded cell - my father went to the chief psychiatrist and threatened to scale the walls of the asylum to free my mother if she wasn't released forthwith.

After the Axeblow

An old gash in a tree-trunk
Made me shiver as the scar
Of a flesh-wound would.

The same quiver ran through me once
When I learned how my orphaned mother
Lost her reason when her first son died.

The gaping scar in the wet bark:
Convulsed lips wailing
After the axe-blow.

For years I struggled to write about our family tragedy without success until fellow songwriter and close friend Paddy Houlahan suggested that I address my dead brother directly in a song. On the night this idea was put to me I had a dream in which I was standing in the portico of a chapel where a line of desks with nameplates attracted my attention. Approaching one of them I noticed that my own name was printed on the plate. While I was puzzling over the inscription I became aware of a male figure in a milky haze standing behind the desk observing me. Because of the mist, I couldn't make out his features but I had the distinct feeling that I was looking at my own deceased brother fully grown.

Inviolate

John Duhan they called me, after you.
O brother the blessing has been a burden too;
Cast in the shadow of your early death
While you remain inviolate.

Two coffins leaving our hall,
Grandad's and yours so white and small.
Father at sea, mother an inmate,
And you remain inviolate –

Free of the strain that weighed on our hearth,
Creating a pain that still tears our home apart.

I once climbed the branches of our old pear tree
And found some hard fruit where none used be.
It tasted bitter, still we all ate,
And you remain inviolate.

Every day after school when I was seven or eight I used to drop into a bar next to our house on Wolfe Tone Street to visit Nancy L, a kind spinster who ran the pub with her slightly dotty brother, Fintan, who fancied himself as a magician. During my visits Nancy always gave me a glass of red lemonade while her not so generous brother, Fintan, would greet me with the single word "Abracadabra" and pull pennies from my ear, which he never gave me.

One afternoon when I went into the bar, Fintan was there alone and there were no customers. Coming from behind the counter with his usual grin, he muttered Abracadabra and told me that he had a new magic trick to show me. Taking me by the hand he led me into a small, dark, windowless storeroom full of wooden porter barrels, telling me that he was going to shut me in and free me without the aid of the key.

After he locked the door, I stood trembling in the pitch black confined space waiting for the door to open, but ages went by and it remained shut. The strong smell of porter started going to my head and made me feel queasy. I tried to force the door open but it wouldn't budge. In a panic, I began to shout Fintan's name as loud as I could and bang on the door with my fists. After a few minutes the door suddenly creaked open and Nancy stood before me with a white face, squeezing her hands. Taking me by the shoulders she calmed me down and explained that Fintan was gone to bed with a bad headache. She then put me sitting on a high stool and gave me a large glass of lemonade.

While I was sipping the fizzy drink through my sobs, Nancy produced a bright coloured flyer advertising Fossett's Circus. As well as tigers, lions, elephants and clowns, there was a pair of acrobats with long poles balancing on a high-wire displayed on the leaflet. Handing it to me, Nancy smiled and offered to take me to the circus the following week, if I didn't tell anyone about Fintan locking me in the store-room. Without hesitation, I agreed and that's how I came to see the high-wire act that gave me the idea years later for the chorus of my next song.

Trying to get the Balance Right

We don't always live in harmony,
Often there are times when we are enemies;
I fight with you and you fight with me
Trying to get the balance right.

Sometimes we cause each other pain,
Sometimes our wills are not the same;
Often we tire of the strain
Of trying to get the balance right.

Like a circus pair high up in the air
Working on their act, we need that kind of pact;
High above the ring, watch them balancing,
See how they unite, we too can get it right.

I know we don't always get along,
One of us often acts too strong,
Sometimes we find we're going wrong
trying to get the balance right.

Like a circus pair high up in the air
Working on their act, we need that kind of pact.
High above the ring watch them balancing,
See how they unite, we too can get it right.

Like many couples, my parents had quite a struggle holding their marriage together because of their conflicting temperaments. When astrology became the vogue some years back I looked up the compatibility of their signs not only in western but also in Chinese astrology, and both systems predicted complete disharmony for such a pairing. Sceptical as I am about such esoteric findings, I remember times growing up when my parents were at such loggerheads I thought their relationship would never survive the strain. In a conversation on marital breakdown with the poet Mary O'Malley I once suggested that the conflict between my parents was so intense at times it was like two stones being knocked together creating sparks that combusted into the fiery dysfunctional family we became. Not withstanding that, after one particularly sulphurous family row, I remember asking my brother Eric rhetorically if he thought it would have been better for all concerned if our parents had divorced or separated years before, and his reply concurred with my own take on the matter: "No, for we wouldn't be here then."

In their old age my parents did find a semblance of the kind of harmony they no doubt had at the beginning of their relationship. I remember visiting them when my father was in his 70s while undergoing dialysis for kidney failure. Three times a week an ambulance called to our house to pick him up early in the day. One morning while I was there, sleeping in a downstairs room, the sound of the ambulance outside my window woke me. Knowing that my father was about to head out for his treatment, I got up to wish him well. As I approached the door which was slightly ajar, I spotted him in the hallway clasped in my mother's arms in the middle of an intense kiss. Instantly I was taken back forty or more years to when I used to see them similarly engaged before my father went back to sea with his knapsack on his back.

The Second Time Around

At 7a.m., he rose from his pillow,
Touched her shoulder and said, "It's time".
She watched him get dressed, then followed him down
To the kitchen in her dressing-gown.

This kind of procedure, they knew it so well
From when he was a sailor returning to sea.
The same heavy feeling came back to assail them
Though he was now seventy three.

Facing the old fears like they used to do
Back in the hard years they had come through,
With all the strength and courage they had found
In the same love still with them the second time around.

After just a sip of tea he rose from the table,
Put on his old topcoat and paced the floor.
She looked on in sympathy over her shoulder
As he moved from window to door.

Facing the old fears like they used to do
Back in the hard years they had come through,
With all the strength and courage they had found
In the same love still with them the second time around.

Just before eight o'clock an ambulance pulled up
Outside our front door, calling for him.
They blessed themselves going out and stopped in the hall
Where she kissed him full on the mouth.

One of my oldest memories – I couldn't have been more than six or seven at the time – is of waking in my parents' bedroom in the dead of night while my mother was in the throes of giving birth. All but two of us were born at home, and as a boy I often slept in my parents' bedroom when my father was away at sea. Though faint and hazy, the recollection is full of soft light, gentle whispers and wall-shadows wavering above my mother's bed while the child was being born. If there were any agony cries from my mother, I don't recall hearing them, though I was aware of the great effort and struggle she was undergoing before the first birth-pangs pierced my ears. Neither my mother nor any of the elders around her luminous bed were aware that I was awake, so still did I remain during the birth. Breathless at the great mystery that was unfolding before my eyes, I remember comparing the wondrous spectacle to the nativity scene at Bethlehem depicted in Christmas cards, holy pictures and the crib in St Joseph's at Christmas time.

Woken Gently

Woken gently in the dead of night
In a candle-lit room,
I turned and saw a wondrous sight
Slip from a womb.

"O Mother Mary" a midwife cried,
"O sweet Christine,
Your child is born,"
The lady sighed by candle gleam.

The flame grew still, the light grew bright,
Our mother beamed with joy
On the glowing presence of her newborn baby boy.

Woken gently in the heart of night
By our father's son.
I saw the struggle, I saw the fight
Our brother won.

The flame grew still, the light grew bright,
Our mother beamed with joy
On the glowing presence of her newborn baby boy.

Woken, mother, at your brightest hour,
I saw you shine
With a pure and gentle power -
Love divine.

Some years back I was invited to take part in a celebratory concert to mark the 20th anniversary of the publishing house Brandon Books soon after the company published my memoir, *There is a Time*. Gerry Adams, the Sinn Fein boss (also published by Brandon) was the star attraction along with one of Ireland's foremost crime writers, Ken Bruen.

Being from the same neck of the woods, Ken and I travelled to Dingle together and made our way to a guesthouse that had been booked for us on the seafront. By an uncanny coincidence, the landlady of the place turned out to be an old Limerick friend of one of my sisters and also the sister of the garda Jerry McCabe who had been murdered by the IRA. Because Ken and I were due to have dinner with a group that included Adams that evening, I felt very awkward in Nuala's company, knowing that she knew who I was going to be sharing a stage with later that night. I also felt very unsettled an hour later going to the pre-concert meal in our publisher's house.

Adams turned out to be the perfect dinner companion, full of jovial stories that kept the table well entertained. At the concert he also read a very moving passage from one of his short stories about a long-term prisoner that he once shared a cell with. He stole the show and drew several encores before I took to the stage to wind up the night with a few songs.

Though he had told me at the dinner table before the concert that he knew several of my songs, I'm not sure if Gerry waited around for my performance. If he did he would have heard me sing a song that I wrote after the birth of our first child, Ronan.

When You Appeared

All the stars were shining,
The moon was climbing
When you appeared.
Your mother and I were smiling,
The doctor was smiling
When you appeared.

But a man was shot down in cold blood
Out in the street, love,
When you appeared.
And somewhere the earth was quaking,
Buildings were shaking
When you appeared.

The lights were bright in the theatre,
Spotlighting your mother
When you appeared.
Your mother was laughing and crying,
Crying and laughing,
When you appeared.

But a man was shot down in cold blood
Out in the street, love,
When you appeared.
And somewhere the earth was quaking,
Buildings were shaking
When you appeared.

Ah but all the stars were shining,
The moon was climbing
When you appeared,
When, love, you appeared.

Children, they say, are the cement that hold a home together. This no doubt is true but I'll never forget the terror that accompanied the joy I felt at the birth of Ronan. It was a stark wake-up call to responsibility. And the demands it placed on my shoulders grew in time.

> In a parting glance outside a railway station
> I saw fear crystallize in my young son's eyes
> and I became more acutely aware of his
> dependence on me. Now I must shoulder
> responsibility, gain courage and strength so
> that when I return I may be more worthy of
> this confidence placed in me.

Twenty five years on, Ronan and his shipmate, Siobhan, became parents themselves a few years back, making Joan and I a couple of proud grandparents.

> Was it six magpies I counted on that tree in my rush
> to early mass? So many I lost count. But later, when
> I phoned Maternity, my timing was spot on: They put
> me straight through to the jubilation of the labour ward
> where the delivery-nurse's high pitched "Congratulations"
> rang out like a consecration-bell as my son Ronan took
> the phone and breathlessly told me of the double
> blessing. Though suddenly a grandfather, my heart rose
> like the sun and fluttered like a bird above a nestful of
> shell fragments, feathers and baby wings.

Aoibheann & Alanna

Aoibheann and Alanna came in spring
When the daffodils appeared.
Three and three magpies spread their wings
And all our world cheered,
And all our world was cheered.

Aoibheann and Alanna twinned in grace –
A double blessing come to light;
One mirroring the other's immaculate face
And eyes so clear and bright,
Eyes clear and bright.

And silently we approached
With smiles and gifts in wonder,
And gently we held and touched
Their bodies frail and tender,
And whispered in our purest tones
Holy thanksgivings
For the healthy flesh and bones
Of our newborn living.

Aoibheann and Alanna one year on,
When the yellow flowers returned,
Brought back the joy, it beamed upon
Their eyes while a candle burned;
While one white candle burned.

Every year while our kids were going to primary school Joan had their photos taken and kept them in a single frame, one behind the other. I came upon her unawares the other night, poring over the full collection with a melancholy look in her eye. Noticing me, she lowered the photos and sighed, "Where have all those years gone?"

Bringing up kids isn't all plain sailing. Our teenage daughter Niamh went off the rails some years back; dropped out of college and started hanging out in some of the shadiest bars in Galway's dockland area. As parents, Joan and I were the last to find out what was going on. When some friends eventually put us in the picture - after they discovered Niamh "flaked out" in their front garden at three o'clock one morning - we were devastated. In a state of bewilderment, we looked at one another trying to figure out where we'd gone wrong. When we couldn't detect any serious fault lines in the way we'd brought her up, we speculated on which side of the family gene pool she stemmed from. Joan reminded me of my alcoholic uncle Jim, who ended up in jail as a petty thief, and I countered by reminding her of a drunken cousin on her side who had been up in court several times for changing the identity tags on the ears of his cattle. In this blame-game we neglected to look at our own past until the penny dropped and Joan reminded me that neither of us had been exactly angels in our heyday.

On a number of occasions while singing my next song on stage I've seen women in the audience dabbing their eyes with handkerchiefs and a few of them have approached me after my performance with stories of their own wayward offspring. With my fingers crossed firmly behind my back, I tell them that our daughter Niamh is now back on the rails and leave them with an adage I heard from an old farmer some years back: "They say the wild ones become the wise ones in the end."

Your Sure Hand

Unravelling fairy-lights for the Christmas tree
On dark frosty nights, do you remember how we
Kept our patience up in tangled wire
Until the tree lit up and you glowed like the fire?
We've not forgotten it was your sure hand
That freed the knots of the most ravelled strands.

Now you are seventeen, moving away,
Still in your tangled teens, what can we say?
We believe in you and we've no doubt
That all you are going through, you will work out.
We've not forgotten it was your sure hand
That freed the knots of the most ravelled strands.

Out in this twisting world when you're confused
Think of the little girl who used
Ingenuity and care
To make a Christmas tree flare.
We've not forgotten it was your sure hand
That freed the knots of the most ravelled strands.

One evening I entered our living-room at dusk and found our nine year old son Kevin standing by the bay window gazing up at a fingernail of moon and a cluster of needle-point stars with a slightly bewildered look on his face, as though he was becoming aware for the first time of the vastness of the cosmos and of our seemingly insignificant place in the broad scheme of things. At the same time I recalled a moment from my own youth, standing with my father at our street corner looking up at a full moon and the Milky Way. What we were doing just standing there, I can't remember, but one of the few books I found in our house while I was growing up was a hardback volume on astronomy that belonged to my grandfather, which my father may have read and which may account for his stargazing that night.

While we were looking skyward, I recall, my father patted me on the head, as if he sensed some unease in me brought on by the mystery of the universe. What he didn't know was that any unease I was feeling that night was brought on not by the complexity of the galaxies but by the fact that it was the end of summer and I was due to return to school to the Christian Brothers in the following days. Despite the misplaced affection, the memory of that pat on the head remained with me. My next song is a pat on the head to Kevin for any unease that may be in his life.

Face the Night

O little boy, don't fear the dark;
Look up in the sky, see it spark;
The Maker's in his forge working away
Shaping another day.

O little man, don't be afraid,
There is a plan heaven-made;
Look at its bright pattern shining above,
Now it's in your eyes, love.

Face the night don't turn away,
The starlight can be much clearer
Than the light of day.

O little one, don't you fear,
The going of the sun has brought the moon here,
With a trail of stars burning like coal
Warming the heart and soul.

Face the night don't turn away,
The starlight can be much clearer
Than the light of day.

Our son Brian was the terror of our estate. As well as breaking a number of our neighbours' windows and trampling on their flowerbeds, he once broke into the Gordens' back-garden and freed their pet rabbit, Snowy, exposing the domesticated creature to the wild fangs of marauding mongrels. In time most of our neighbours – including some of our closest friends – came to view Brian with dread and suspicion.

In stark contrast, Willie D – a boy who lived close to me when I was growing up – was a model of politeness and good behaviour, praised by every mother on our street. And you could see why. Always dressed to the nines in neatly pressed suits with shiny shoes and prim hair, Willy looked the picture of respectability and good manners. Rarely coming out to play, he was said to spend at least three hours doing his homework after school each day. And every evening without fail – while the rest of us tearaways would be playing handball or football on the street - Willy would link his widowed mother, bent double from arthritis, to evening Benediction in St Joseph's, making sure never to out-step her snail's pace.

For years Willy kept up this grim routine, rarely speaking more than a word or two to any of the kids on the street. Then one Sunday morning out of the blue he approached me while I was tapping a ball against Beegans' gable and asked me – as cool as a cucumber – if I would like to join him in stealing a bag of collection money from a drawer in the priory of St Joseph's chapel after twelve o'clock mass.

What became of Willy in later life I have no idea (though I wouldn't be surprised if he ended up in jail). As for Brian, he outgrew his delinquent ways and has lately taken up short story writing as a hobby, which didn't surprise me, as he once helped me to write my next song when he was no more than five or six.

So like me, our little boy; he bounces a ball
while I try to write. Then I tire of the sense
I'm trying to make and he tires of his game
and cries for my pen. Now I'm bouncing the
ball and he's happy again. What's he up to
at all?

Brian's Song

The light comes back to me
And shines radiantly above a girl and boy
Whose eyes are bright with joy,
Whose eyes are bright with joy.

It's the morning part of day;
Sunlight on the bay dances in their eyes
While above the Atlantic noise
Their voices start to rise:

Brian begins, then Ailbhe sings, and I join in:
It's the morning and the sun is in the sky,
A bright morning and boats are sailing by;
It's morning and our hearts are riding high
On the crest of a wave.

Brian's song comes back to me
With a sweet melody; and again we're on the band
Of road to Silver Strand;
See the rocks, the sea and the sand.

Though our daughter Ailbhe gets a mention in Brian's Song, she griped for years that she was the only one of our kids who didn't have a song written exclusively for her, until I put her in the bridge section of my next lyric.

Ireland (For Ailbhe)

On this rock I sit for the joy of it,
Watching the Atlantic's uplifting waves,
Ireland.

Here in Galway Bay just the other day
An old woman turned to me with fear in her eyes,
Ireland.

Ireland, our land; a sacred island
Facing America - on shifting sand,
Ireland.

Now I gaze around the shore
Wondering what's in store for our daughter,
Who is running in the sand
Holding out her hand towards the water.

I look out to sea where it's all hazy;
I pray, still uplifted on this rock,
Ireland.

I was in our local supermarket with Joan some time back when a sales rep distributing free chicken samples told me that she was a big fan of one of my love songs. Noticing the name Mary M pinned on her uniform, Joan later told me that she had recognised the rep as the wife of a newscaster at our local radio station, Galway Bay FM. After this initial contact Mary M pulled us up on a number of other occasions when we went shopping – once while she was giving out cheese bites and another while distributing cocktail sausages – and each time she complemented me on my love song.

This went on over a four week period and then one day Joan arrived home with a grave expression and told me that she had just heard a presenter on her car radio offering condolences to his colleague at the news-desk on the sudden demise of Mary M. At first the name didn't register with me till Joan elaborated: "You know, the blonde at the supermarket who gives out the freebees, the girl who's a big fan of yours." I shook my head in disbelief. "Was a big fan, you mean."

As it happened, I was playing a show that night in a nearby arts centre. During the gig I told the audience about the deceased sales rep and dedicated her favourite love song to the memory of her departed soul. There wasn't a dry eye in the house.

The following Friday (our regular shopping day), Joan and I were back in our local supermarket with a trolley-full of groceries, steering down the frozen foods aisle, when who should we run into only Mary M in a ghost-white uniform standing behind a pan of sizzling fish-fingers. Luckily there was a large group of shoppers sampling her goods so she didn't notice the look of amazement on our faces as we wheeled by with our trolley.

After making some discreet inquiries from another member of the supermarket staff we discovered that Mary M's husband's mother shared the same Christian name as his wife, and it was for her passing away that the radio presenter had offered his condolences on air.

We've Come Through the Night

We've come through the night,
Now it's growing bright;
A rift in the curtain is letting in light,
Making it clear we're still near.

This home we own
Gains colour and tone;
The beat of your heart gives life to the stone,
So first thing each day I pray -

To a crack in the ceiling overhead
With tender feelings for you in this bed,
So our relations withstand the strain
That shake the foundations where we have lain,
Where love is lain.

Some shadow remains,
A lingering stain
Left from the dark with a shade of the pain
That fades away as I pray -

To that crack in the ceiling overhead
With tender feelings for you in this bed,
So our relations withstand the strain
That shakes the foundations where we have lain,
Where love is lain.

We've come through the night.

I was strolling through Barna Woods one afternoon when a man stopped me and told me that he was a big fan of my work. "Yeah" he enthused, "I have a few of your albums, but I have to say, one song of yours really gets on my wick, The Voyage. It's too sugary and takes the sailing metaphor too far, especially with that duff line about the relationship."

Agreeing that I might have overdone it a bit with this one word, I went on chatting and asked the man if I was right in detecting a Cork lilt in his tone. Admitting that he originally "hailed" from the banks of the Lee, he confessed that he hadn't been back in Cork since his mother's funeral more than twenty years before. Curious to know what had kept him away from his homeplace for so long, I asked him if there was a reason for the long absence . He hesitated for a moment then told me that he had no wish to visit his brothers and sisters because he felt nothing but "hate" for them. The word hate sent a shiver down my spine and later made me reflect on the less extreme divisions in our own extended family.

In Our Father's Name

In the long shadow of our family tree
That darkened once the heart in me
I found good reason to believe
In our frail seed.

And in our children's eyes I watch it grow
As I watched it once in the early glow
Of my brothers' and sisters' eyes
Before our broken ties.

Our roots run deep in sorrow
And will hurt as much tomorrow
If we don't try to end the blame
And restore peace, in our father's name.

O the silver birch near our home
Embedded in black earth and stone,
Its branches lean together on high
In the clear blue sky.

Our roots run deep in sorrow
And will hurt as much tomorrow
If we don't try to end the blame
And restore peace, in our Father's name.

In the long long shadow of our family tree
That darkened once the heart in me
I found good reason to believe
In our frail seed.

Introduction to Chapter Four

In this final chapter I struggle to carry a torch with a weak hand. **Flame** is not a collection of devotional songs but a series of strains that struggle against a rising tide of doubt.

RTE produced a series of radio programmes some time back outlining inconsistencies in the Bible. Week after week a tetchy broadcaster fulminated against the wonderful old stories we all grew up with, dismissing them as fantasy. Had he taken the trouble to read Augustine's Confessions, the disgruntled presenter might have saved himself a lot of trouble, as they too tell of the bafflement Augustine encountered reading a literal interpretation into scripture until Ambrose put him on the figurative trail.

Pascal's famous wager on God's existence was turned on its head by the French poet Mallarme, who, acting on the same chance principle, opted not to believe. Soon after he dispensed with God, Mallarme came to the conclusion that poetry isn't about meaning and compensated for his loss of faith in a system that had given birth to most of the artistic wonders of the world by devising a fresh approach to poetics through elliptical rather than spiritual means. Other poets followed in his wake and produced poetry as exotic as shells washed up on Dover beach, objects beautiful to behold but devoid of lasting life.

Dante railed against poets who use "rhetorical ornament without meaning". And closer to home, Cardinal Newman warned that "heresy can...be an enlargement of the mind" that leads astray.

When God ordered Abraham to leave his birthplace for a new homeland, Abraham acted on faith and was rewarded with prospects beyond his wildest dreams. In this chapter, I strive to follow in Abraham's footsteps, even if I do so with a wobbly step.

Chapter Four

Flame

I remember as a boy sitting by the fire
pondering on a dark night
and my mother's warm voice saying to me,
"You're a dreamer! God only knows
what you see in those flames."
When darkness falls around me now,
I do it just the same – sit by the fire
and look for the glow of warm words
for what God only knows.

Before going to the States some years back I tore up a whole sheaf of half-baked songs - years of work - that didn't measure up to honest scrutiny. New York shook the cobwebs from my brain, set my nerves tingling and got my creative juices flowing again. "Only by suffering the rat-race in the arena can the heart learn to beat," observed Rilke and Keats came to a similar conclusion: "Do you not see how necessary a world of pain and trouble is to school an intelligence and make it a soul."

In The Afterbirth

A baby born in blood
Cries out as it should,
For where there's life there's pain,
So the soul will gain.

A mother looking on
Sheds happy tears upon
The child who hurt her so,
So the soul will grow.

Creation's mystery
Come down through history;
Its trail upon the Earth
In the afterbirth.

A mother has no rest;
The infant at her breast
Demands all she can give,
So the soul will live.

Creation's mystery
Come down through history;
Its trail upon the Earth
In the afterbirth.

In the early eighties I went over the edge after being dropped by yet another record company on the eve of the international release of my first solo album. For months I couldn't sleep or eat or think properly. At my lowest ebb I looked in the mirror and a famine victim stared back at me. I prayed to the God I didn't believe in at the time to "pull the wool back over my eyes" so that I might go on with my life, but the nightmare went on and on. By this stage I was completely disillusioned with almost every aspect of the popular music industry, believing that the whole rotten ethos should be abandoned like the communist ideology that was beginning to crumble in Eastern Europe at this time. In my heart I knew that a lot of the bitterness I was feeling was sour grapes for all the failure I'd been through, but I didn't know how to overcome the rancour that was eating me alive.

The Blight

With the blight on my mind
The poison ran straight to my heart;
Then I couldn't find courage
To make a fresh start;
I had worked many years on my own,
Clearing deadwood in a western zone,
But for all of my effort my brain turned to desert
Where the buzzards wouldn't leave me alone;
I lost almost three stone,
Eaten with worry I was picked to the bone.

For six months or more
I was consumed with despair;
I locked my front door
And wouldn't go out anywhere;
At night I was tossed in my bed
By a fever going on in my head;
I was famished and weak and I found little sleep
And the little I found full of dread;
My dreams were all fed
On that terrible blight that wanted me dead.

With my eyes dripping tears
I knelt down one day and I prayed.
Hadn't done this in years
And it made me no less afraid;
That night was no better for me,
No let up in anxiety,
But at dawn in the sunlight someone called me outside
And out there I started to see
In a mist from the sea
Among my own neighbours
There were others like me.

On the morning The Blight came to me - after weeks of rooting for a way into the song - I picked up Pascal's *Pensees* and randomly opened the volume on this passage from the Book of Amos: "...I will send a famine on the land, not a famine of bread, nor a thirst for water, but of hearing the word of God..."

I had returned to practising my religious faith just before this time. It wasn't a big transition. Whereas before I lived in occasional doubt of my unbelief I now began to live in occasional doubt of my belief - a subtle change but one that I hope will make all the difference in the end. One noticeable improvement in my day to day existence was that I began to see that reality faced squarely can be far more beneficial than the stuff of dreams.

Just before I wrote my song After the Dream I teamed up with a character who had all the cunning and charming characteristics of a real Sancho Panza. Though Peter Harkin's history was even more chequered with mishap and failure than my own (he was a rehabilitated drug-user on his way to becoming an alcoholic when we met) he had an unwavering belief in the providential that allowed him a rock-solid faith that every endeavour he turned his hand to was preordained to succeed. Even when nine times out of ten his pipe-dreams led him astray, he quickly recovered his confidence and composure and went off chasing some other harebrained scheme with just as much enthusiasm as before. The lowest point in our collaboration came when Pete booked me into a club in a remote part of Co Waterford without a money guarantee, on the pie-in-the-sky basis that we would take one hundred percent of the door. I warned him that this was a risky thing to do, but, using his considerable persuasive powers, he convinced me that the club owner's assurance that the venue had a regular crowd was true and that the gig was going to yield us a small fortune. Three people showed up on the night and two of them had driven forty miles from a neighbouring county to see me.

On the way home from that cancellation (the only one in my long career) Pete confided in me (after some probing) that his big dream in life was to become a photographer, which he eventually became with great success.

Despite his flagrant incompetence as a booking agent, Pete landed me one of the best jobs of my career - a commission to score the music for Joe Comerford's film *Reefer and the Model,* which featured After The Dream and went on to win top prize at the Barcelona Film Festival.

All through those sleepless nights
while my restless heart hammered away
in the dark like a working forge,
sparks flew heavenward outside my window,
but I hardly noticed them till one morning
I looked eastward and, by my soul,
saw the heart of day rise up in burninshed gold.

After the Dream

In the night I had a dream,
It felt so right I thought it real,
Then I awoke and it was gone
But in its place I found the sun.

I had a girl, a lovely girl,
In my life she was my world,
Then one day I found her gone
But in her place a truer one.

I had a prayer I used to say,
A simple prayer for night and day;
As I grew, I forgot the words
But now I find they've returned:

In the night I had a dream,
It felt so right I thought it real,
Then I awoke and it was gone
But in its place I found the sun.

To mark the anniversary of the brutal murder of a group of Jesuit priests in El Salvador, I was asked to sing my next song outside the American Embassy in Dublin a few weeks before I was due to apply for a visa to visit the States.

Conditions weren't ideal on the day of the protest; it was raining cats and dogs and there was a mad breeze rattling the placards outside the embassy. Beneath a priest's extended brolly with my guitar strapped around my neck and my son Ronan standing by my side, I glanced up at the lit windows of the circular embassy building, noticing the stars & stripes flapping through the corner of my eye, and I started singing at the top of my voice while hoping that I wasn't being photographed for CIA files.

Christy Moore featured a version of El Salvador on his **Ride On** album. After that, other popular Irish singers started recording my songs. Maybe it was coincidental, but this change in my fortunes coincided with my return to practising my Christian faith.

When I turned on my TV
A Cyclops was looking at me.

El Salvador

A girl cries out in the early morning,
Woken by the sound of a gun;
She knows somewhere someone is dying,
Bleeding in the rising sun.
Outside the window of her cabana
Shadows are full of her fear;
She knows her lover is out there somewhere –
He's been fighting now for a year
To heal the soul of El Salvador.

The moon like a skull is over the country,
The sky to the east is blood-red.
A general wakes up and takes his coffee
While he sits on his bed.
Outside the barracks soldiers are marching back
With their guns in their hands;
The general goes out, salutes his army,
And issues new commands;
He makes the guns roar in El Salvador.

Bells ring out in a chapel steeple;
A priest prepares to say mass.
A sad congregation come tired and hungry
To pray their troubles will pass.
Meanwhile the sun rises over the dusty streets
Where the bodies are found;
Flies and mosquitoes are drinking from pools of
blood
Where a crowd gathers round;
They cry for the soul of El Salvador.

Set on a hill with a spire like a mast
and a regular bell, the chapel sits
like a ship gone aground in a swell.

Midsummer Night
(In memory of Tom Stenson)

Jade in the amber glow of a streetlight,
the tree stood out majestically on the misty hill
on midsummer night in front of the angular silhouette
of the Church of the Resurrection.
Beneath the brightening stars it looked exotic,
almost too rich for a poor neighborhood like ours.
This impression was transitory, however, as the
imperial look owed more to the mist and shadow
than to any lasting reality. While my eyes were feasting
on its momentary glory, I thought of all the poor
families in their semis by their tellies. I thought
of their darkened altar. Then I turned away and knelt
to pray.

I started attending daily mass in the mid eighties, almost against
my will at first, as I knew that the practice was out of step
with many of my contemporaries who had long since deserted
religion. Going to the chapel on the hill was often a lonely
experience, especially midweek when the entire congregation
consisted of no more than a handful of elders. Once as I was
taking my place in my customary pew near the back of the
almost empty church the thought struck me that I attracted
more of an audience to my poorly attended gigs than our parish
priest drew to his weekday services, despite the fact that he was
one of the finest priests in the city.

Fr Lawless

Your name
belies the order
that the Word
on your tongue
has brought
to our lives.

Religious practice – which included a fairly strict regime of contemplation, prayer, fasting and spiritual reading - made me reassess my life, and from the revaluation evolved the plan to formulate my work through spiritual guidelines. I had always believed in inspiration (though I was never quite sure of its origin) but now I deliberately began to pray for divine assistance in a systematic way. And my prayers were answered. Though I had a backlog of sixty or seventy unrecorded songs (not counting the hundreds, if not thousands, of rejects dispensed with along the way), there was no clear order to the collection. Now that began to change. After a false start of recording **Family Album** (the first edition of The Voyage collection) for an Irish record company that demanded an input into shaping the work as part of their investment, I broke free during the recording of **Just Another Town** (as already related) and fashioned the first edition of that series at my own expense, without compromise.

Though **Just Another Town** received some harsh criticism from pop and rock journalists when it was first released, it later gained higher praise than I could ever have imagined from the highly respected writer and broadcaster John MacKenna in an RTE documentary, Songpeople. Outside of the artistic accomplishment of the individual songs, John saw that what made the collection work as a whole was the cohesive theme of community that underscored the work.

Soon after I produced **Just Another Town** - and as a direct consequences of reflecting on the community aspect of the work - I joined a charitable organization and started visiting the poor and disadvantaged.

In Thoughts of Others

On stormy nights on muddy route
To visitations – rain-soaked and wind-lashed –
I've often wondered why we do it.
At worst we're duped by those we help,
at best we do them little good.
But there's also the almost selfish reason
that informs the heart even in the hardest weather
of the peace we gain when we forget ourselves
in thoughts of others.

One young woman that my co-worker, Mary, and I started calling on was Mona, a lone parent of three children whose estranged partner, Norman, was just out of jail after a two year stretch for burglary and aggravated assault. Though Mona had taken out a barring order on "Norm", he started breaking into her council house and beating her up whenever the drunken whim took him. Eventually, the police managed to warn him off and he stopped tormenting the poor woman. For two or three months we gave Mona a sympathetic ear and a little financial assistance. And when her mental state improved, we stopped calling on her.

A year went by and Mona contacted us again, seeking financial help after the birth of a new child. Presuming that she'd patched things up with Norm, we called on her in some trepidation and discovered that she had a new man in her life – "Dickey", a shady looking character who greeted us with a defensive assurance (unasked for) that he was unemployed. After a brief interview with Mona, we agreed to assist her for a few months and started calling with food vouchers every Monday night. During this time we made the grim discovery that Dickey had another family in a nearby estate whom he divided his time with, as well as owning his own apartment in a different part of town. Puzzled as to know how he could afford to support three households on social welfare, we made some discreet inquiries and learned that Dickey was a small time drug peddler. Concerned for the children, we confronted Mona with the discovery but she flatly denied that either she or Dickey had any involvement with drugs. After some more probing, our suspicions were confirmed that Dickey was in fact involved in the drug trade (on a small scale) but when we broached the subject with Mona again, she became confrontational and told us to "fuck off" out of her house.

Months went by and we heard nothing more of Mona. Then one frosty mid-December afternoon while we were distributing Christmas hampers to other poor families in the neighbourhohood we paid Mona a courtesy call to wish her seasonable greetings and found her in dire straits, strung out on drugs, almost oblivious of her gaunt-faced children huddled together beneath grubby blankets in an ice-cold room that looked like it hadn't been cleaned in months.

We helped the family out over the festive season, but soon after Christmas, Mona's four children were taken into state care and Mona was warned that she wouldn't get them back until she went through an extensive rehab course, which she reluctantly agreed to do.

After six or seven months of attending this programme, Mona's children were returned to the family home and Mona slowly started rebuilding her life, with Dickey out of the equation.

Over the years, we have assisted countless other families in similar circumstances, but one poor soul slipped through our net, due to my misguided priorities.

A Man

A man I saw regularly
drinking wine beneath a bridge
on my steady way to church
jumped in the river and drowned.
Now, in my mind, I often find myself
standing by the water's edge,
talking to the man long after
the last bell has stopped ringing.

When still in my mid twenties - after years of struggling to get a foothold in the music business - I wrote my first batch of half decent songs and recorded them with an Italian/American producer I connected with in London. While Steve V went off to Los Angelus with the master tapes to cut the deal, I moved to Joan's parents' farm for what I imagined would be a brief respite. Three weeks later I received a wire from LA informing me that the deal was in the bag but that Steve was going to need me to sign fifty percent of my songwriting royalties over to him for perpetuity before he would send me the flight tickets for Joan and myself. Needless to say, I turned him down flatly and consequently ended up stuck in a boggy rut in Co Galway for over two years. At my lowest ebb I went for a walk to a desolate pond on the edge of a heathery wilderness with our oatmeal Labrador, Sancho. The pond was frozen over with a thick crust of midwinter ice. I threw a stick out on the glassy surface for Sancho to retrieve and, while I was watching him making his unsteady way across the ice, I recalled another frozen pond that I myself had walked on with a friend when I was nine or ten as part of a boyhood dare. Though we were aware that another boy had drowned while skating on the same frozen pond a few years earlier, we recklessly went ahead and tiptoed out onto the brittle ice. After a few faltering steps my nervous companion chickened out and turned tail, while I, show-off that I was, stuck my neck out and forged ahead. As I neared the centre, the ice began to sizzle and crack beneath my feet. For a moment I thought my number was up but somehow I managed to get back to solid ground before the pond went to pieces. Recalling the thrill of the risk and the hot slaps of congratulations I received from my friends when I got back to terra firma, I marvelled at my own youthful courage.

Thinking back on this in the shaky state I was in after the collapse of my LA deal, I wondered if I still had any of the old bravado left in me. To test my metal, I stepped onto the edge of the pond and stamped on the ice a few times to gauge its firmness. Close by, with the stick in his drooling mouth, Sancho eyed me curiously, as if to say, "Surely you're not going to be fool enough to try a stunt like that!" When the ice didn't crack under my pounding pressure, I took a few tentative steps towards the centre, gaining confidence the further I went. Quarter way out the ice started cracking and breaking up at my feet and, before I knew it, I started sinking in the freezing cold water. As I went down I remembered being told by Joan's brother, Paddy, some time before that the pond was bottomless - a piece of local folk-lore that I was relieved to discover was nothing but myth. When the water reached my chin my feet touched base and I sprang back through a range of shattering ice shards to the frosty bank, where Sancho, still ogling me with the drooling stick between his teeth, shook his head, as if to say, "Serves you right, fool!" With chattering teeth and icicles forming at my knees and elbows, I made my way back down the bog road to the cottage where I found Joan's mother, Mary-Dear, plucking a goose in the farmyard outside the back door. Through a cloud of grey feathers she scrutinised my stiff, shivering frame and laughed. "Masha, what happened to you, a maneen; did you fall in a bog-hole or what?" While at the back of her mind she was probably thinking: Masha, what kind of a gombeen has me daughter teamed up with at all?

Notwithstanding this mishap, the memory of my boyhood courage, along with a new set of songs, eventually helped kick-start my career again, and years later, during another marooned stretch on the rocks, the memory of the same youthful incident gave me the idea for an epic song on my misadventures.

On the Water

I walked as a boy out on deep frozen water;
I did it 'cause I was dared to try like Peter.
And where his heart failed,
Mine prevailed despite the danger;
I knew this entailed
Death if I failed, still I took the wager.

As I grew to a man I didn't change in my nature;
I developed no plan to secure a future;
At sixteen I left school, broke every rule,
Ignored all the censure;
When warned that the world was cruel,
I acted cool and left on adventure.

As I travelled around I followed the road without fear,
But soon I found reason enough for tears;
In a grubby old bed, hungry for bread
And weighed down with care,
Clutching my head in fear and dread,
I learned of despair..

Then I met a girl, she brightened my world and I loved her.
But she felt in peril on the pedestal where I put her;
With no head for such heights, she lived in fright
Of my heavy nature;
There were passionate fights till she left one night
And went with another.

In my reckless career I've been a fool and a sinner;
When temptation was near I risked my soul to be a winner;
In my lust for gain I caused someone pain
Who didn't recover;
The act left a stain – the mark of Cain,
I came to discover.

O yes I've been all at sea in mutiny with my father,
And the spirit in me felt hopelessly in danger;
My faith ran dry, it started to die
And I started to falter;
But then I thought of the boy who dared to try
To walk on water.

Yes I walked as a boy out on deep frozen water.

Singing those six long verses without the relief of a chorus can
almost be as hazardous as the act of walking on the ice itself,
but whenever I manage to reach the end without slipping up
I'm rewarded with a thrill almost equal to the feeling of getting
off the ice alive.

Audience response has always been important to me at live shows. I love getting feedback at the end of my gigs. However, when the response comes while I'm still on stage it's a different matter.

One night in The Red Lion in Lower Manhattan (a pub/restaurant venue where the clientele's main focus is on food and drink rather than musical entertainment), I opened my set with a joke: "It's great to be here in The Red Lion but, with all this chewing and swallowing going on in front of me, I feel a bit like that Biblical character Daniel - you know, the guy who was thrown into the lion pit for saying his prayers." When only a few people laughed, I knew I was in for an uphill battle.

After my opening song, a burly guy in the restaurant area shouted up a request for Song Sung Blue. When I told him I didn't do covers he became obstreperous. Half way through the first verse of my second number – a song about my uncle Jim – the chubby guy pointed his steak knife at me and burped: "Who cares about dead-beats. How about giving us something we know, buddy?" I lost my temper at that stage and became obstreperous myself. "Hey Tubs," I hissed into the mic, "why don't you stuff some steak into your mouth and let me get on with my job!" This went down a treat with a sizeable section of the audience, but the owner of the venue wasn't impressed. During my first break he called me aside and gave me a dressing down: "You can finish your next set and I'll pay you. But you'll never work here again!"

Though I wouldn't have accepted a second night in the place anyway, I felt desperate after the show, as this was just one in a line of similar bum gigs I'd played in the weeks gone by. On my way to a friend's apartment in New Jersey where I was staying that night, I experienced a feeling of mental and spiritual collapse.

Morning Star

A twofaced clock in a distant tower
Harshly struck an ungodly hour;
I was out of luck and feeling sour,
With time running out.

I stumbled and cursed and sat on my case,
My heart fit to burst in that lonely place;
I cried in my thirst for some kind of grace
To ease my doubt.

There in the dark I couldn't see
There was a spark overhead me
Beginning to burn for the day
That was coming my way,
Coming my way.

The clock struck again, I got to my feet,
Raised my chin and looked down the street;
There were no other men; no, no one to meet;
I walked on.

Minutes after I received a phone call from my sister telling me that my father had only days to live, I had another call, from my wife just out from our GP with confirmation that she was pregnant. Torn between conflicting emotions, I caught the first bus home and spent the following days in vigil at my father's bedside with my mother and brothers and sisters.

After one particularly harrowing sleepless night, I walked to the Shannon at dawn just in time to witness a spectacular sunrise. A pale moon was fading in a pink and turquoise sky above Cleaves' Bank and the river was so still it was hard to tell where the water reflections ended and the real landscape began. Mesmerised by the beauty of the place (there were swans and doves floating out on the misty river that brought angels to mind), I stood transfixed for a few moments but then my father came back to me in his fusty old bed and I began to feel how unfair it was that nature should remain so fresh and vibrant while we humans, after our brief span, grow old and die.

I walked down the quay and came to a familiar mooring bollard that instantly took me back to a moment in my boyhood when I stood in the same spot with my father when he was still a young man. He was pointing towards a narrow rowing boat manned by seven or eight young oarsmen going upriver against the flow, and he said, "I must take you to the next regatta and you'll see lots of boats like that racing." The word "regatta" lodged in my mind like a magic charm that I played with for the rest of that day, trying to decode its hidden promise. When my father eventually did take me to my first regatta I wasn't disappointed. It was on a clear summer's day and there was coloured bunting – lines and lines of red, yellow and green triangular flags flapping in the breeze – all along the quayside, where crowds of onlookers cheered on the competing boats.

With this memory in mind, I returned home and found my father propped up in bed, quite conscious. I touched his wizened hand and told him about my walk to the river. His eyes lit up and a huge smile enveloped his face.

The River Returning

From the raft of his dying bed
My father smiled at me
When I returned from the river
And told him it looked heavenly,
Shining in the bright sun at the break of day
With a full moon above it spiriting it away
To the deep, deep ocean; the wide, wide sea -
The river returning, flowing free.

On the wharf that morning
Down the sunny quay,
I found an old bollard
And moored to it the memory
Of me and my father in a moment of joy
Just watching together the Shannon going by -
To the deep, deep ocean, the wide, wide sea -
The river returning, flowing free.

My father's dying
Brought back to me
His days as a sailor
Returning to sea,
And once when he left us and sailed away
How I tried to follow him as a stowaway
To the deep, deep ocean; the wide, wide sea -
The river returning, flowing free.

Before my father's funeral I walked to the Shannon again. It was a damp misty morning and my head was muzzy after having stayed up half the night *waking* my father with family and friends. During the course of our tipsy trip down memory lane - while others were commending my father for the stoicism of his acceptance of his final illness - I praised him rather for the strength and forbearance he had displayed after the crippling blow fate had dealt him as a young man when his son and father had died on the same day and his wife had ended up in a mental hospital.

With this tragedy resurfacing in my fuzzy mind, I stood on the "whistling bridge" gazing down river and noticed a cormorant bobbing on the choppy water, about to dive.

Requiem

It was a black morning.
A cormorant dived below
the surface of the Shannon
and re-emerged with a flatfish
in its bill.
              The bell was tolling
for my father's funeral mass,
but I was held spellbound
on the bridge, caught by the pall-
black sight of the bird
swallowing the fish.

In drizzling rain while I and my brothers were shouldering the coffin to the graveside - where a priest was standing with dangling rosary-beads - I recalled a joke my father had cracked when I made the surprise discovery that he had taken up the practice of dropping into St Joseph's to pray on his way home from work: "I'm still as sceptical as ever about an afterlife, but you know me, a gambling man; I'm just hedging my bets on the off chance that your mother might be right."

Ulysses' Last Voyage

The monotony of the hometown
finally sickened him, so he left again,
in a narrow wooden vessel.
On our heaving shoulders
He floated all the way to the brim,
then sank without a trace.

It had been a long held ambition of mine to write music for a mass but I could never pluck up the courage to attempt the challenge, aware as I am of the vast canon of hymns and chant that already exists in the wide portals of sacred music. Then out of the blue one day I had a phone call from the chairperson of the Bereavement Committee of University Hospital Galway, Margaret Duignan, who asked me if I would sing at a commemorative mass for the deceased staff members of the hospital.

In some trepidation I took on the commission on the basis that I would be given a free hand to come up with the music and lyrics myself. With a deadline of just four or five weeks, I set about my task and after many false starts I found a taper of inspiration for my opener.

The Flame is Lit

The flame is lit,
The table's set for supper.
The guests are here;
Gathered, we're together.
The ruby wine's mature,
The bread baked white and pure
We will savour.
We have come to eat
A spiritual meat
With our neighbour.

Our thoughts are on
Loved ones gone before us.
A heavy price, Christ's sacrifice,
Restores us.
In the sharing of this meal
And through our shared ordeal
There is union,
Through the Holy Ghost
Who revives a broken Host
In Communion.

The flame is lit,
The table's set for supper.

For the psalm, I chose No. 62, and felt very puffed at the idea of sharing the credits with one of my favourite songwriters of all time.

> My soul is thirsting for God,
> For God I'm thirsting.
>
> Like a desert, my soul is dry,
> I long for waters from on high.
>
> In the sanctuary, Your glory ablaze,
> On your pure love I gaze.
>
> All my life, my hands I raise,
> For your banquet I give praise.
>
> Beneath the span of your night-wing,
> On my bed I muse on You and sing:
>
> My soul is thirsting for my God,
> Thirsting for God.

In lieu of the Lord's Prayer, I resurrected a song I'd written some years before which dealt with my shaky return to the faith.

Surrender

Before my final surrender,
Before I finally gave in,
I worked by night, kept up the fight,
Thinking my way might still win;
But at dawn I was finally captured
As the sun came over the hill,
I lay down my arms and surrendered my will.

As I was taken prisoner,
I thought I heard a loud shell
Over my head where the sky was blood-red,
It was the sound of a bell;
And the chapel where it was ringing
Was right on top of the hill;
Inside a choir was singing of God's will:

"Thy kingdom come, Thy will be done
On earth as in Heaven."

As I was led to the summit,
I thought of the battles behind,
Some of them lost at such a high cost
To my heart and my mind,
But a padre there to meet me
Right on top of the hill,
He said my defeat was victory, as God's will.

When Margaret first approached me to sing at the mass, she specifically asked for a Marian hymn. Soon after this, our daughter Niamh visited us with her newborn baby prior to the infant's christening. I was so taken by the beam in the child's big blue eyes, I though of writing a song for her. A melody came to me but when I tried to put words to it, I hit a brick wall. After countless failed attempts I was about to give up when the thought occurred to me to try and apply the melody to the concept of a Marian song, and straight away the idea ignited.

Because the Virgin birth had puzzled me since my youth - after my father had sown the seed of doubt in my mind about immaculate conception - I couldn't figure out where the inspiration for the lyric had come from until I focused on the opening line and found the DNA for the entire song in the words "mystic blue". By allowing for a figurative interpretation of the miraculous event, the lyric developed in a fresh way.

I was so overwhelmed by the quality of the melody and poetry, I tried to figure out its creative process in my song journal:

> I can't stop singing The Burning Word, which proves to me that it's the real thing. The verse section, in musical terms, is very sweet, and then some slight dissonance comes into the chorus - I'm not quite sure how tech-nically - even though the chord structure remains simple. Whatever happens, the change in tone is perfectly in tune with the words' disturbance…..

> A long time ago I prayed for the inspiration for a group of faith songs – and I remember asking specifically that they be simple and self-contained, so that they would be musically and poetically effective even played on a single instrument. That wish has been granted in the almost perfect form of this little hymn to Mary. As I say, I can't stop singing it. And I need to go on singing it because, though short, it's quite an intricate song to perform on the guitar while singing. But I love singing it.

The Burning Word
(For Katey)

An angel came to you
Out of the mystic blue
While you were praying to
God above.

Pure as a lily flower
Closed in its petalled tower,
You opened to the power
Of love.

Though pain would ensue
From the flame that burned in you
Still you embraced the burning Word.

The angel flew away
After he had his say
On that most sacred day
For Love.

Gabriel came to you
Out of the mystic blue
While you were praying to
God above.

Dipping into my past again, I found a song I'd written about the Israelites' forty years sojourn in the wilderness as punishment for their disobedience and impatience with God. The inspiration for the song was partly fuelled by my own long career of going nowhere with just the love of family and friends to sustain me. But overriding all this, the song is a hymn to the spirit of community.

Part of a Tribe

How did we survive the last forty years
With all those trials,
Going round in circles for all those miles,
How did we ever survive?

As part of a tribe we respected each other,
The law was inscribed that we love one another
And though it wasn't always applied
The law never died.

How did we revive, when we despaired
When our faith died,
When we lost our courage, when we wept and cried,
How did we ever revive?

As part of a tribe we respected each other,
The law was inscribed that we love one another,
And though it wasn't always applied
The law never died.

How did we thrive with all the confusion
Going on in our minds,
And all the destruction that we left behind,
How did we ever thrive?

As part of a tribe, etc.

A priest once told me that I shouldn't feel guilty about practicing my religious duties during periods of doubt, or even when my faith was almost extinct. I'm very grateful to that man. So, for him and for all doubting Thomases, I dedicate this final song of the mass, which came to me literally on the eve of the service.

Sure Amen

Our Father above
fired with love
lighted as a dove
on Jesus.

No love greater than
the love he brought to man,
dying in his plan
to save us.

And when He rose again
He told us broken men
to sing a sure amen to Heaven.

Amen, Amen, Amen.

Our father of grace
You showed the human race
your loving face
in Jesus.

The lonely tears he cried
showed his human side
before he bled and died
for us.

And when He rose again
He told us doubtful men
to sing a sure amen to Heaven.

The Bereavement mass was held in the tiny chapel of University College Hospital Galway on the 5th of November 2005 before a congregation of less than a hundred. Having barely made the deadline, I sang the songs solo at the side of the small altar, reading the lyrics and straining over my guitar to remember the chords. At the end of the mass the presiding priest, Fr Tommy, praised my efforts and the assembly gave me a warm round of applause. After that, I went home thinking that that was the end of it.

A few days later I received an invitation to sing the songs again in Lourdes for a group called the Notre Dame Invalid Trust. The highlight of the visit was to be a mass at the very site of the apparition. The thought of singing The Burning Word at the famous grotto swayed me into accepting the offer straight away.

As it transpired, the mass scheduled to be said at the Marian shrine where Bernadette saw Our Lady was cancelled soon after we arrived in Lourdes, due to over demand by other invalid groups. But this didn't matter once our group started the daily trek of processions to the various holy sites with our cavalcade of wheelchairs. The vast crowds of disabled and sick we rubbed shoulders with at every turn along the way took my mind off the superficial reason that had brought me there in the first place, and it slowly began to dawn on me that the real attraction of Lourdes is to be found in the wounded eyes of the hordes of crippled pilgrims who gravitate from all over the world for the illusive cure and miraculously find solace and consolation in one another's prayerful company.

Towards the end of the six day pilgrimage, I was having a glass of wine one evening with my roommate, Tommy, in the hotel patio when a toddler from the Children's Invalid Group – Joey, a young boy who up till this time had been covered in bandages - jumped up on my knees calling me "the song man" - and started showing me his clear-skinned arms and legs while boasting that his eczema had been cured by "the holy waters"at the grotto. Noticing his mother close by, I felt very uncomfortable having him on my lap, not only because child abuse scandals were rampant at this time but also because I wasn't sure if his rare form of eczema was contagious. Looking into his lively eyes, I felt ashamed of my feelings, but this didn't stop me from putting him down. Standing beside me, Joey went on displaying his healthy limbs – which for years, according to the children's nurse, had been covered in bleeding sores. Eventually his mother came over and told him not to be bothering us. With a radiant look on her face, she confirmed that her son had been cured and told us that she was hoping and praying that the "miracle" would last. After she and Joey went back to their table, I gave Tommy a sceptical look and said, "It's amazing what the power of the mind can do!"

The following morning at breakfast Joey's cure was the main topic of conversation. While we were munching croissants and sipping tea my fellow diners expressed optimistic hope that Joey really was cured, but level headed nurse Mary suggested that we "wait and see".

On the final day of the pilgrimage the "miracle boy" was involved in another near miraculous incident. While showing his arms and legs to another patient – a frail anorexic – he asked her if she was aware that everyone in our group was talking about how thin she was. Up until this time the young woman in question had been in total denial about her almost skeletal condition – taking only water and tea at meal times – but Joey's innocent remark brought home to her for the first time the real emaciated state she was in.

My light is propped precariously
on Pascal's *Pensees*, St Augustine's *Confessions*,
and on St John of the Cross's *Dark Night of the Soul*.

Captain

O Captain, I'm sharing your raft;
My Jesus, just two beams attached;
And my heart's in my mouth 'cause I'm full of doubt
And you're looking so bloody and grey
Stretched on the timber that way.

Yet you kept me going when my faith was low
With stories of mystical places you know
Where wretches like me might finally go
If we don't sink down too low.

O Captain, my soul's all at sea;
O Christ, won't you please answer me;
And I swear I'll obey whatever you say
But I can't even hear your heart beat
Lying at your bleeding feet.

Yet you kept me going when my faith was low
With stories of mystical places you know
Where wretches like me might finally go
If we don't sink down too low.

O Captain. my hope's almost dead;
O Christ, and you're still dripping red,
And I feel so alone in monotone;
O why can't you do what you say
And rise up and show me the way.

I was rushing past a Franciscan church on my way to a railway station to catch a train when I spotted a perfectly good coat lying on some steps outside the friary. Cautiously, I picked it up and put it on and continued my hurried journey. The fact that the garment wasn't mine began to bother me, so I searched the pockets in an attempt to locate any documentation that might indicate the owner of the coat. In an inside (heart-side) pocket I found a leather pouch containing a chain-watch without the chain. While studying the watch, I arrived at a station I'd been in before. I woke at that juncture and jotted the details of this dream into my song journal, which, after some reflection, became a song.

The Coat

Take this coat and put it on you
On this autumn day;
It will keep you warm and dry
While it's wet and grey.
I found it near a chapel
In a vivid dream;
Faith the fabric of this jacket,
Doubt not it is clean.

Take this coat, it's like another
My mother gave me
When I was just a boy
And faith a mystery.
I wore it to the chapel
On the Father's hill
O the fabric of that jacket
I am wearing still.

Take this coat now, I implore you,
And put it on;
It is damp outside and cold,
And summer is long gone.
You might wear it to the chapel
At the bell-sound;
Faith the fabric of this jacket
Found on holy ground.

On our way to midnight mass one frosty Christmas Eve - I was no more than seven or eight at the time - my mother and brothers and sisters and I were held up in the portico of the church by a decrepit old woman on walking sticks being helped into the chapel. As we approached, I observed her wizened face enmeshed in a network of deep wrinkles, and I shuddered. When we got inside the church I turned to my mother – still in the smooth-skinned bloom of her twenties – and implored her never to grow old.

I reminded her of this while holding her bony prune-like hand in Inisgile Nursing Home some months before she died.

When You Go

This world made you sad;
Took the bright dreams you had
And woke you on dark mornings
To worries and warnings.

But I know when you go,
In the life hereafter,
You'll be there without a care
And the angels will fill you with laughter;
I know when you die,
Though we'll sit and cry,
You'll be at peace, your pain will cease
And your spirit will begin to fly
When you die.

This world made you sweat
And filled your heart with regret;
For each pleasure you've paid double
In tears and trouble,

But I know when you go,
In the life hereafter,
You'll be there without a care
And the angels will fill you with laughter;
I know when you die,
Though we'll sit and cry
You'll be at peace, your pain will cease
And your spirit will begin to fly
When you die.

On the morning my mother died I drove to the hospital and sat by her bed. While praying, I was struck by the expression on her face. The upward thrust of her features reminded me of a bird about to take flight. I took solace from this, imagining that she was straining heaven-ward at the time of her departure

When I got back to Galway, I walked the narrow pathway by the golf links in Salthill, close to the rocky seashore. The tide was fully in. I found a spot among some rocks and sat gazing out over Galway Bay. The Atlantic was as calm as I'd ever seen it. Little wavelets curled onto the shingle in front of me, making gentle hissing sounds like breath being exhaled. A feeling of total tranquility came over me and I began to imagine that the stillness of the day was somehow connected to the fact that my mother was now finally at peace after her long turbulent life.

The squeal of a low-flying gull pierced the silence. I turned and watched the bird hovering above some barnacle-covered rocks at the water's edge. Another gull flew in and fluttered above the first bird, then both of them flew off together. I recalled a dream my mother had told me about some weeks before in which my dead father was calling to her. I smiled and got to my feet.

The bird-like expression on my mother's face in her death-bed came back to me. I picked up a stone and threw it into the sea. A ripple arched towards me from the splash. As I watched it grow into a perfect circle a boyhood memory came back to me in which I arrived home with an injured pigeon. My mother let me keep the bird in our shed, where I nursed it back to health.

After recalling this, I headed back along the pathway, glancing at a golfer on the golf links. A couple of small birds flew over my head and perched on the mesh fence dividing the path from the green, whistling and flapping their wings. The golfer took a shot but all my attention was on the two little joyful birds.

Months later I received a package in the post from John Griffin containing several poems and a moving story about his mother. The title of one of the poems caught my attention. I asked John if I could adopt it for a song, and he agreed.

Song of the Bird (For John Griffin)

She let him nurse a frail bird
With a broken wing;
She gave him bread for the bird
And the bird began to sing.
She came alive in the boy
Who now hungers for the word
To tell the world of the joy
Of the song of the bird.
And so I sing to the world
Of what was heard in the song of the bird.

She lost her mother as a child
And as an orphan bride
She lost a son. She lost her mind
And her spirit all but died.
But she came alive in the boy
Who now hungers for the word
To tell the world of the joy
Of the song of the bird.
And so I sing to the world
Of what was heard in the song of the bird.

She gave him faith in the Sun
He gave her hope in the light.
And now he prays, as a son,
For her song to take flight.
For she came alive in the boy
Who now hungers for the word
To tell the world of the joy
Of the song of the bird.
And so I sing to the world
Of what was heard in the song of the bird.

Unless we go live in the North Pole for a section of the year, we have to accept that night follows day and that a high proportion of our time in this world has to be spent in the dark, literally and metaphorically. But this isn't necessarily a bad thing. With the aid of modern technology, astronomers have recently trained their highly sophisticated lenses on an area of the cosmos known as the Deep Field that was once thought to contain nothing but black empty space and there they discovered myriads of bright galaxies multicoloured as meadows of summer flowers.

The Dark Side

I have looked at the dark side of life.
As well as day I've studied the night.
While others slept and dreamed it was bright,
I have looked at the dark side of life.

I have trembled with fear in the dark.
I've confronted old ghosts with my heart.
And each one accused me and gave me a start,
I have trembled with fear in the dark.

Night can be black, blacker than coal,
When there's cloud in the way.
But when that cloud rolls back other worlds unfold
That you can't see by day,
Other worlds you can't see by day.

I have walked through the shadows of night;
And in the dark I feared for my life.
Where each passer-by might carry a knife,
I have walked through the shadows of night

Some years back my wife Joan invited a teenage nephew of hers to come and live with us while he was establishing himself in a new job in Galway. Though I quite liked Davy, I found his impish nature very irritating at times. Often while I'd be working in the evening, he'd breeze into my room and look over my shoulder at my lyric in progress, saying, "Is that a new one, John Pon? Looks good. I'd say you'll get a fair few royalties from that when it comes out." Or, "You're looking happy today, John Pon. You must have got another big royalty cheque. How much?"

I'm not sure where the "Pon" came from but I found it very annoying. In time I learned to put up with Davy's impudence but one thing I couldn't grow accustomed to was his habit of usurping the remote control for the TV each night and zapping around the channels from my favourite armchair while I struggled to get access to the news from a hard chair behind him.

After months of putting up with this strained state of affairs, I lost my rag one night and told Davy to find new lodgings. Joan thought this measure over-harsh (she doted on her nephew) so I ended up having a flaming row with her also. That night I went to bed feeling wretched and woke early the following morning with a guilty conscience. To try and regain my equilibrium, I rose before dawn in the winter chill and put myself through a rigorous course of contemplation that culminated in a breath-taking experience.

All At Once

The air was cold, the room was dark;
I was shivering and fear gripped my heart;
So I called out your name
And I called it over again.

I knew I'd hurt you by what I'd said;
My tactless words went round in my head,
So I called out your name
And I called it over again.

Then all at once a warming flame
Heated my blood when you came.

The air grew warm, the room grew bright.
Then morning broke the grip of the night,
So I sing out your name
And I'll sing it over and over again.

After reading a newspaper review of one of my albums in which the lyrics of several of the songs were misquoted and denigrated by a journalist I'd had a row with several years before, I wrote a letter of protest to his editor with the carefully designed intent of getting him into serious trouble. On the advice of my prudent better half I held back before going to the post office and then began having second thoughts about sending the barbed letter. In a weak moment I tried to strike a bargain with God, offering to tear up the complaint if the Holy Spirit sent me the inspiration to complete the final verse of a song I was having great difficulty with (over a three year period I wrote hundreds if not thousands of failed verses). Realising that I was engaged in in trying to bribe the higher powers, I came to my senses and threw the bitter letter into the fire. Early the next day an old memory came into my head that sparked off an idea. I picked up my pen half abstractedly and without strain or effort the complicated rhyming structure of the illusive final verse ignited like fire in my head and then blossomed like a flower on my page.

I turned and stared into her gleaming eyes.
She smiled shyly and moved in in the bed.
I stepped towards her, breathing in the rose
scented air, telling her that some day I would
write her a far far better song.

Flame

A rose won't grow
If the soil below goes dry,
It withers and droops and dies at the root,
And its red petals drop
Like blood that won't stop from a wound
And then the flower
Without any power lies ruined.

The heart is the same,
The stream in the vein gives it life;
Cut off the flow and it won't go
For blood is the source
Of all that force in the beat;
Body and soul
Need it to roll for heat.

And fire won't glow
If wind doesn't blow on the hearth;
The yellow blaze
Smoulders and fades,
And you're left to poke
At the cinders and smoke that remain,
But without air
You would despair of the flame.

O when my first flame died
And you became my love
A fresh breath of air made sparks appear
And my heart, like coal,
Lit up and my soul took fire,
While out in your bed
You grew blushing red, my flower.

"If poetry comes not as naturally as the leaves to the trees it had better not come at all," noted Keats. But before leaves appear roots have to toil long and hard below the surface, as the American poet Theodore Roethke observed in his wonderful little poem Cuttings, which marks the great struggle that the "lopped limbs" and "dry sticks" of plants make before buds can spread their wings.

Before I found a way into my final lyric I had to literally uproot myself and fly across the Atlantic.

In New York I ran into fellow songster Jimmy McCarthy at the Irish stand of a global music seminar in Manhattan's famous Marquee Marquise hotel and the first thing he said to me was, "We've come to the mountain!"

Disliking the mart-like atmosphere of the place, I left after an hour and, later that same day, I went into a second-hand New Jersey bookshop and the first book I picked up was *Ascent of the Mountain, Flight of the Dove* by Michael Novak. Thinking back on Jimmy's solemn remark I was tempted to buy it but, sceptical as I am of serendipity, I put it back on the shelf despite the low $3 price tag on the tail of the dove. Two weeks later, back in Jersey visiting Tom Prendergast, I went into the same bookshop and straight away spotted the same book. Opening it, I was surprised to find that the first chapter was The Voyage, the title of one of my most popular songs. Smiling at the extended coincidence but still guided by my own natural scepticism, I was about to put the book back on the shelf when I noticed that the price tag had been reduced to $1.50. Laughing at myself, I forked out my buck and half and threw the book in my case when I got back to my apartment, putting off reading it till I returned home to Ireland.

Soon after I arrived home my father fell ill and died. Just before he passed away a strong melody came to me while I was sitting in vigil at his bedside - a present, I like to think, from his departing soul. I tried to write a lyric around it based on the struggles of my father's life, but it didn't work. Then I got the idea of writing about the uphill slog of life in general. At the same time, I started reading *Ascent of the Mountain, Flight of the Dove*, which turned out to be close in theme to the subject I had in mind. As always when ideas for lyrics come to me, I went to my song journal and started keeping notes that might help me find a way into the song, in the same way that artists do sketches for major paintings. At first I groped around in the dark like a character from a short piece I once wrote to describe my awkward approach to songwriting:

> I'm still playing blindman's buff,
> stumbling and falling while using my mind;
> it's more by feeling, I find.

Days, nights, and weeks of stumbling and falling while feeling my way into the knotty substance of my final lyric went by before the memory of a simple family outing set me on a track up a mountain - or glorified hill - behind Kylemore Abbey in Connemara.

The Beacon

When we saw the white beacon
Near the top of the hill,
The children stopped their fighting
And went suddenly still,
And before we brought the engine to a stop
They said, "Please let's climb that mountain to the top."

We parked the car by the old Abbey
And found a narrow path
Winding up the hillside
So we followed that.
We met people coming down with smiling faces
Whose bright eyes revealed they'd been in higher places.

Then the children grew more daring
And went climbing on ahead.
Soon we couldn't see them,
So we listened hard instead;
Our wild angels started calling through the bracken
And put our minds at rest. Our pace didn't slacken.

Over stumps, stones, mould and boulders;
Over rock-ledges and -shelves,
We struggled on and upwards
And rose above ourselves;
And we weren't even wearing heavy boots,
Through our soles we could feel real living roots.

And we thought of the first pilgrims
Who forged that narrow track
Up that rugged hill-face
With the beacon on their backs.
And as we strained over the last ridge to the summit
We wondered how they ever could have done it,

Till standing there before us
High above the rocky moss
We found a silent answer
In the figure on the cross,
And our breathless children looking on were saying,
"It's so clear up here" which sounded just like praying.

Song Index